A TEACHER… …OOLKIT for TEACHING OLDER LITERATURE

SUE HACKMAN
JO SHACKLETON

Hodder & Stoughton
A MEMBER OF THE HODDER HEADLINE GROUP

Acknowledgements

The publisher would like to thank the following for permission to use copyright illustrations:

The British Film Institute (p. 16); Charles Keeping/Oxford University Press (p. 59); © BBC Worldwide (p. 65)

Every effort has been made to contact the holders of copyright material but if any have been inadvertently overlooked, the publisher will be pleased to make the necessary alterations at the first opportunity.

Orders: please contact Bookpoint Ltd, 39 Milton Park, Abingdon, Oxon OX14 4TD. Telephone: (44) 01235 400414, Fax: (44) 01235 400454. Lines are open from 9.00–6.00, Monday to Saturday, with a 24 hour message answering service. Email address: orders@bookpoint.co.uk

British Library Cataloguing in Publication Data
A catalogue record for this title is available from The British Library

ISBN 0 340 70524 8

First published 1998
Impression number 10 9 8 7 6 5 4 3 2 1
Year 2004 2003 2002 2001 2000 1999 1998

Cover photographs: Brontës © The National Portrait Gallery; Illustration by Cruickshank © Bridgeman Art Library.

Typeset by Fakenham Photosetting Ltd, Fakenham, Norfolk.
Printed in Great Britain for Hodder & Stoughton Educational, a division of Hodder Headline Plc, 338 Euston Road, London NW1 3BH by Redwood Books Ltd, Trowbridge, Wiltshire.

CONTENTS

INTRODUCTION

Why read older literature?

> 'The past is a foreign country: they do things differently there.'
> (*The Go-Between*: L. P. Hartley)

Older texts have stood the test of time. Generations of readers have found in them things to delight the imagination and interest the intellect. A book which can sustain delight over the centuries is worth a second look.

Older texts can take us under the skin of generations who lived before us. A turn of phrase, a leap of syntax or a subtle choice of vocabulary can bring to life for us the attitudes and feelings of people who lived before us, and put us in sudden intimate contact with the past.

One of the chief pleasures and difficulties of teaching older literature is that it immerses the reader in a world which is only half familiar. This includes the language. Students need time to attune to the distant voices of writers whose language is similar to, but different from, our own. It is unwise to defer the teaching of pre-1900 texts until they are older, and perhaps more 'ready'. Only experience will make them ready. Little wonder that students approach older writers with trepidation and disinclination: if they have little or no experience of older texts then their first encounter with older texts is intimidating: the language looks unfamiliar and off-putting.

The best course of action is to introduce older literature into the curriculum at a much earlier stage. Younger students are surprisingly receptive to older literature; they do not have the taboos of fear and awe which students acquire as they move through school. The names of Shakespeare and Dickens hold no terrors for them. We need to provide exciting and interesting experiences of older literature for students as soon as they are able to enjoy it. Otherwise we risk inadvertently depriving them of the things that would make it accessible to them - confidence and familiarity.

Older texts are part of the diversity which children need to progress as readers. They need wide experience if they are to generalise from their reading, becoming versatile in their reading strategies and discriminating in their choices. They need to experience writers of different cultures, genders and periods in order to understand what is special about each of them.

When students leave school, many of them never take up older literature of their own accord. If we defer the experience because we believe they are not ready, they will never be ready. No-one else will introduce it to them. Teachers represent the best chance they have of a secure introduction to the treasure chest of literature written by previous generations.

In this book, we hope to demonstrate how teachers can meet the challenge of teaching older literature without compromising sound educational practice.

There is nothing here which has not been tried and tested in the classroom and found to be successful. We hope you will find it useful and inspiring.

FIG 1 Writers through the ages

From the top (left to right): Jane Austen; Charles Dickens; William Wordsworth; William Blake; William Shakespeare; Christina Rossetti; the Brontës; George Eliot; Thomas Hardy.

CHAPTER 1

Older literature across Key Stages 3 and 4

LONG TERM PLANNING

The National Curriculum for English requires teachers to plan over two key stages since the requirements of Key Stages 3 and 4 are currently combined. Many English Departments have realised the flexibility this offers and have tailored their curriculum planning to suit individual departmental and school needs.

The reading requirements in terms of heritage literature are quite specific so you will need to map the reading curriculum for your students. A useful starting point might be your chosen GCSE syllabus since some of the texts you choose will be dictated by examination set lists and coursework requirements. Once these are in place, it will become easier to plan the reading curriculum for Years 7, 8 and 9, in order to ensure not only that the National Curriculum requirements have been met, but also that differentiation and progression have been fully considered. The English Department stock cupboard may well be your starting point and you may be surprised at how much material you already have which can be revitalised. However, if you are short of suitable older literature, you may need to target capitation accordingly over the next few years.

Choice of texts and teaching strategies will vary from school to school and within departments, but the long term plan should offer an aerial map of the reading curriculum you intend to deliver.

In the plan below, pre-1900 texts are highlighted to show how they have been integrated into the curriculum map:

	First half term	**Second half term**
Autumn term Yr 7	MODERN NOVEL	STORYTELLING – modern short stories – oral tradition – folk tales
Spring term Yr 7	PLAY SCRIPTING – group reading, performance and scripting	SCHOOL UNIT – writing for a range of audience and purpose
Summer term Yr 7	PERSONAL WRITING – diaries and journals – biography and autobiography – travel writing	CRAFTING POETRY
Autumn term Yr 8	NOVEL – *Treasure Island* by Robert Louis Stevenson	SHORT STORY GENRES – *The Tell Tale Heart* by Edgar Allan Poe (horror)

		– *The Speckled Band* by Conan-Doyle (crime) – *Tony Kytes, The Arch Deceiver* by Hardy (romance)
Spring term Yr 8	LANGUAGE VARIETY – accent, dialect, SE	VILLAGE PROJECT – writing for variety/audience
Summer term Yr 8	RESPONDING TO POETRY – *La Belle Dame sans Merci (Keats)* – *Isabella (Keats)* – *The Tyger (Blake)* – *The Clod and the Pebble (Blake)*	INTRODUCING SHAKESPEARE – *Extracts from 3 plays*
Autumn term Yr 9	WIDER READING	VIEWS OF LONDON – *Diary entries from Pepys* – *Upon Westminster Bridge* by Wordsworth – *Dickens – book box*
Spring term Yr 9	SHAKESPEARE – *Romeo and Juliet*	CLASS CAMPAIGN
Summer term Yr 9	THEMATIC STUDY: – adolescence	MEDIA UNIT
Autumn term Yr 10	POST 1900 POETRY	PRE 1900 PROSE – *Jane Eyre* or – *The Mayor of Casterbridge*
Spring term Yr 10	POST 1900 DRAMA	POST 1900 PROSE
Summer term Yr 10	PRE 1900 DRAMA – *Macbeth*	PERSONAL WRITING
Autumn term Yr 11	PRE 1900 POETRY – *Rossetti* – *Tennyson* – *Browning*	PERSONAL WRITING
Spring term Yr 11	REVISION OF EXAM TESTS	GCSE PRE RELEASE ANTHOLOGY – *Some older pieces*
Summer term Yr 11	EXAMINATION	

MEDIUM TERM PLANNING – PREPARING A GAME PLAN

The medium term teaching plan is basically a game plan of how you are going to teach the text. It is designed to cover a block of time such as a term or a half term. The medium term plan is an important document for the department. It should be easy to share: although the teaching intentions are defined, there is still room for individuals to manoeuvre, organising the kind of activities they prefer and teaching them in their own way. It is a useful tool for the department moving away from the 'do-it-yourself' curriculum but wary of the 'do-it-my-way' curriculum.

There are two stages in devising a game plan:

Firstly, section the text by breaking it down into substantial sections. In a longer Victorian novel these might be the original instalments. Alternatively, the shifts of plot, the number of weeks available for teaching, or even the writer's own segmentation might prompt you here. Thus it might be a phrase in the story, or an act in a play or a canto in a long poem.

For example, here are the sections we might use for *The Mayor of Casterbridge*:

Mayor of Casterbridge

INTRODUCTORY:	chapters 1 & 2
SETTING THE SCENE:	chapters 3-13
THE PLOT THICKENS:	chapters 14-25
REVERSAL OF FORTUNE:	chapters 26-35
DISGRACE:	chapters 36-39
TRAGEDY:	chapters 40-45

Secondly, identify the teaching priorities for each section, giving deep thought to the two or three key points you can address in each section. These will be your teaching priorities.

The text will suggest some of the priorities to you, but also take into consideration the needs of the class and the opportunities you know you will have in the future. For example, you won't have many better opportunities to discuss symbolism than the pig's head scene in *Lord of the Flies* but there will be other opportunities to discuss characterisation. It is a matter of seizing the optimum moment.

Many teachers find it difficult to relinquish the many teaching opportunities offered by a rich text. The text beckons, and the examination threatens. But there is no end to what we might teach; every archaic word, every historical reference, every nuance, every literary flourish could be examined. But it is a mistake to do so.

We have to make priorities if students are to have lessons which are pacy and pertinent. We have to clear spaces for students to think, reflect and learn, and to do this we have to teach aspects of literature once, but well. Students have to be encouraged and trusted to apply new insights for themselves. We can remind and revisit but they must learn to use the skills we teach them. The only alternative is to teach each chapter exhaustively and run the risk of overloading them.

Here are the priorities we might identify for *The Mayor of Casterbridge*:

The Mayor of Casterbridge

INTRODUCTORY: CHAPTERS 1 & 2

- to engage interest in book
- to generate first responses
- to identify qualities of a good opening

SETTING THE SCENE: CHAPTERS 3–13

- to establish the central characters
- to secure an understanding of and interest in the plot
- to create a mental image of the time and place

THE PLOT THICKENS: CHAPTERS 14–25

- to notice the role of women characters
- to compare and contrast the key characters
- to appreciate the twists and turns of the plot

REVERSAL OF FORTUNE: CHAPTERS 26–35

- to hypothesise about the possible outcomes of the plot
- to pick out key themes and issues
- to discuss the nature of tragedy

DISGRACE: CHAPTERS 36–39

- to analyse a pivotal scene
- to generalise about English society as it is depicted
- to feel and understand empathy

TRAGEDY: CHAPTERS 40–45

- to respond to the ending
- to consider the job of the writer in ending a novel
- to reflect on the moral justice of the ending

SHORT TERM PLANNING

The short term plan sets out how activities will be organised in the classroom. It may well take the form of brief lesson plans or an approach spelt out in stages. If you plan a text in chunks, it may be convenient to cover one section in the short term plan. The plan will be developed directly from your game plan.

We suggest working from your stated priorities. Consider what it is that students will do to demonstrate, practise or apply this learning. In other words, what will be the outcomes for each section of text?

For example, the priorities for the first section of *The Mayor of Casterbridge* were to engage students' interest in the book, generate first responses and to identify the qualities of a good opening. This might suggest these outcomes:

The Mayor of Casterbridge

Key outcomes for the introductory section: chapters 1 & 2

- reading journals commenced
- shared impressions in groups
- list of features of good opening

At this point, you will also need to plan classroom approaches and teaching strategies. These, along with activities which work well with older texts, are discussed in the next two chapters of this book. However, a short term plan for teaching the first section of this text might look like this:

The Mayor of Casterbridge: Teaching plan for Week 1

Task	Organisation	Key questions/teaching points/learning outcomes
Read, discuss and improvise the extract from the wife-selling scene	Mixed groups, feeding into a plenary debriefing.	• what it reveals about the characters • what led up to it • where it may go from here • where and when set • why in the opening
Introduce the set text	Plenary	• what do we know about Hardy? • whereabouts is the wife-selling scene? • what might this first bit be about?
Read Chapter 1 and start reading journals by responding to periodic questions	Plenary sessions punctuated by individual jotting in reading journal, feeding into whole-class discussion.	• first impressions – man, woman, time, place, local people and where do they come from? • writer's style – key features? • what happens next? Why think that?
Read Chapter 2 and jot down descriptions of Henchard onto a silhouette drawn on A3 paper: his own thoughts and feelings on the inside and the reader's views on the outside. Affix to wall. **Homework**: write a paragraph describing Henchard to someone who doesn't know him.	In ability groups. Circulate in groups around the posters on the wall, and update own silhouette.	• factual information about Henchard • his reactions to the night before • his character as it is revealed • personal reactions to him
Draw out the features of a good opening. **Homework**: next to each feature, find an example from the opening chapters of the set text	Individual entry in journal on what interests/disappoints about this opening. Share in groups. Compose a full list on board.	• set plot rolling • introduce key characters • establish time, place • establish mood, relationship with author • grip the reader • make the reader curious about what happens next

At the end of the planning process, you should be able to see clear links between the long, medium and short term plans. A major assignment in the short term plan - an essay on settings for example, might well be seen as a priority topic in the medium term plan.

CHAPTER 2

Teaching the longer text

USING A READING SCHEDULE

You will need a plan for getting through the longer text. The teaching opportunities are infinite, and never matched by the kind of time one would like, so it is essential to consider your time budget and then allocate sections of the text to fit it. It is simple to divide the text into sections which fit the number of weeks available. It will also bring you down to earth. Time is short, and having priorities will help you to decide which passages to select, how long you can give to each task and how much students will have to do for themselves.

You might decide, for example, to lavish time on the first two or three chapters of a novel by reading them in class to secure a good introduction. But this will mean that later on in the novel you will have to claw back the time by asking students to read substantial sections alone for homework, or by ushering them quickly through one of the sections. There are additional advantages of having a reading schedule, not least that it is useful for support staff, students and their parents.

A reading schedule tells students when you will be dealing with certain sections of the text and which are the key passages for study. It commits your planning to paper for the benefit of the students and those who support them.

The schedule can be handed out as a leaflet or as a poster on the classroom wall. The more able can read ahead and prepare passages in advance for the lesson, and the less able can focus their energies by reading just the priority passages. Some of them who become 'hooked' can read between passages.

Organise helpers to record the priority passages onto tape so that poor readers and absentees have a useful back-up resource.

The example on pp. 10–12 shows a reading schedule for *Pride and Prejudice* by Jane Austen. Priority passages are specified for less confident readers. This particular schedule was designed for use with a mixed-ability Year 11 class. Students were asked to prepare the specified passages in advance of the lesson, and sixth formers read them onto tape for the use of weaker readers.

A word of caution though – schedules can be a constraint. There is not a lot of time to deviate into interesting discussions which arise during the reading, and the timetable is easily disrupted by field trips and unforeseen events. If this happens, you must decide between sticking to the schedule or revising it. The other risk is that brighter students will use the priority passages to minimise their workload.

Reading Schedule – Pride and Prejudice

Week 1
September 1st
Chapters 1–6

The opening chapter
pp. 51–53

The ball
pp. 58–63
pp. 'Mr Bennet had soon . . . to purchase.'

Darcy admires Elizabeth
pp. 70–74
'occupied in observing . . . her wit flowed long.'

Week 2
September 7th
Chapters 7–12

Jane at Netherfield
pp. 78–83
'My dearest Lizzie . . . vulgar relations.'

Darcy & Elizabeth together
pp. 96–98
'After playing . . . that evening.'

Leavetaking
pp. 104–105
Chapter 12

Week 3
September 14th
Chapters 13–19

Mr Collins
pp. 106–110
Chapter 13

More about Mr Collins
pp. 114–116
'Mr Collins was not . . . with his friend.'

Mr Wickham
pp. 120–122
'Mr Wickham was the happy man . . . intelligible gallantry.'

The ball
pp. 133–138
'She danced next . . . as I did before.'

The Bennet family at the ball
pp. 141–144
'In vain . . . rejoiced in it.'

Mr Collins proposes
pp. 146–153
'The next day . . . feeling any regret.'

Week 4
September 21st
Chapters 20–26

An engagement
pp. 165–166
'The possibility . . . she had chosen.'

Thinking about the future
pp. 170–171
'Mr Collins returned . . . said Mr Bennet.'

Miss Bingley's letter
pp. 172–176
Chapter 24

The Gardiners talk about their acquaintances
pp. 180–182
'Mr Gardiner stayed a week ... in Hertfordshire.'

Week 5
September 28th
Chapters 27–34

Visiting Charlotte
pp. 191–194
'At length ... next day.'

Visiting Rosings
pp. 196–201
'In spite of ... his own hands.'

Darcy proposes
pp. 204–226
'Elizabeth had scarcely ... out of sight.'

Week 6
October 5th
Chapters 35–40

Darcy's letter
pp. 229–237
'The part which I acted ... unfit for conversation.'

Lydia
pp. 246–248
'It was the second week ... come back, Lizzy.'

Jane's state of mind
pp. 254–256
'She was now ... on me.'

Week 7
October 12th
Chapters 41–45

Concern about Lydia
pp. 257–258
'The rapture ... rest of her life.'

Elizabeth meets Wickham
pp. 260–261
'On the very last day ... never meeting again.'

At Pemberley
pp. 265–273
'The period of ... how to account for it.'

Darcy's sister
p. 281
'Miss Darcy ... evident enough.'

Elizabeth's feelings
pp. 284–285
'Of Mr Darcy ... his addresses.'

Week 8
October 19th
Chapters 46–52

Bad news
pp. 291–295
'They had just ... must be in vain.'

Lydia's letter
p. 307
The letter.

Mr Collins' letter
pp. 312–313
The letter.

Mr Gardiner's letter
pp. 317–319
'My dear brother … imprudence forgotten.'

A wedding
pp. 331–332
'La! You are so strange! … had been intended.'

Elizabeth reflects on Darcy
pp. 337–339
'The contents … very much.'

Week 9
November 2nd
Chapters 53–57

Bingley and Darcy make some visits
pp. 344–357
'There is a gentleman … a very happy woman.'

Lady de Bourgh
pp. 363–366
'As soon as … no promise of the kind.'

Week 10
November 9th
Chapters 58–61

A proposal
pp. 347–377
'Instead of … ashamed of it.'

An engagement
pp. 381–387
Chapter 59.

An ending
pp. 393–396
The final chapter.

WAYS IN

First encounters with the text are important. Some students will be expecting the text to be difficult, stuffy and inaccessible because it is old. If the text is to make a good first impression, it must inspire interest and confidence. Some texts have great openings and the best tactic is to dive in with a spirited reading, but there are alternatives.

Heralding the text

Whet students' appetites by offering sneak previews of the text: intriguing snippets which appear on the classroom wall, reviewers' comments on the notice board or appetisers from the text read aloud at the end of lessons during the previous week. See Figure 2.

Improvisation of a key issue

Give the circumstances of a key issue in the text such as Macbeth's ambivalence towards Duncan or Jane Eyre's dilemma over whether or not she

FIG 2 A noticeboard on Keats

If poetry comes not as naturally as the leaves to a tree, it had better not come at all.

From a letter

His life was for the most part wretched: he had fallen in love with a Hampstead girl, Fanny Browne, and his poverty and ill-health forbade all thought of marriage. Indeed, it soon became clear that he would not outlive another winter....

Critic J H Walsh

A winter in England would, I have not a doubt, kill me; so I have resolved to go to Italy... for, I think, there is a core of disease in me not easy to pull out.... If I should die ... do not, my dear, tease yourself about me. You must think of my faults as lightly as you can.

From a letter

John Keats – died 23 February 1821, aged 25. Keats died of consumption – tuberculosis – a disease which could be cured today by antibiotics.

Oh, God! God! God! Every thing I have that reminds me of her goes through me like a spear. The silk lining she put in my travelling cap scalds my head. My imagination is horribly vivid about her – I see her – I hear her. There is nothing in the world to divert me from her a moment. O that I could be buried near where she lives! I am afraid to write to her – even to hear of her any how, to see her name written would be more than I can bear. My dear Brown, what am I to do?

From a letter

To Autumn
Season of mists and mellow fruitfulness...

From a poem

She dwells with Beauty – Beauty that must die.

From a poem

A thing of beauty is a joy for ever: Its loveliness increases; it will never Pass into nothingness

From a poem

Fanatics have their dreams

From a poem

Keats never was, nor ever would be, a popular poet.

Written by the poet Percy Bysshe Shelley

should become Rochester's mistress. Ask the students to discuss the issues, improvise the scene or work through the possible lines of development.

A key moment

Why start at the beginning? There can be advantages in starting with a pivotal moment in the text such as the marriage service in *Jane Eyre* or the theft of the gold in *Silas Marner* or the sleepwalking scene in *Macbeth* (see Figure 3). Students can be asked to speculate about what led up to these events and where they might lead.

Appraisal and prediction

Ask students to appraise the cover of the book, taking in its blurb, length, density and title. Invite them to dip in and predict what the book might be about, and how these impressions are formed.

Using video

Show students the opening credits of a film version of the text. Ask them for their predictions. Alternatively, show them the first few minutes of two different versions and ask them to compare and contrast, saying which they prefer and why. Opening credits to Austen and Dickens serialisations are often loaded with a particular view of the text as a 'classic' and it is always interesting to see how scriptwriters choose a story which does not start with action in its original form. Contrasting openings to Shakespeare productions are also illuminating. *The Merchant of Venice* and *Twelfth Night* are good examples.

Sampling activity

Select a number of interesting paragraphs from the full length of the text and ask students to read them closely, put them in sequence and hypothesise about the plot and genre.

The example from *Treasure Island* (see Figure 5) makes use of fragments of different texts such as letters, logs and maps.

KEEPING EVERYONE ABOARD

Once the text is under way, you will need strategies to support the less able readers. The reading schedule has already been mentioned, but you may wish to consider one of the following if it suits the text.

Abridgement

Abridged texts are shortened but retain the original language. **Simplified** texts are quite different since they do not use the language of the original and therefore miss the point of studying older literature. **Abridged** versions retain

FIG 3 Worksheet for the opening of *Macbeth*

THIS IS WHAT YOU KNOW ABOUT THE MAN MACBETH:

1 He is a great warrior – brave, skilful and fearless.
2 He has killed many men in battle – some in the most horrible ways.
3 He is helping the king to put down a rebellion.
4 The king thinks of him as a 'worthy gentleman'.
5 He is a close relative of the king.
6 He is rising higher and higher in the ranks, and is now very powerful.
7 He has just been given a new title.
8 Three evil witches have an interest in him.

IMAGINE YOURSELF IN MACBETH'S POSITION:

- What things about your life might gratify you?
- What might be the limitations or irritations of your position in life?
- What interest might the witches have in a man like Macbeth?

THIS IS WHAT YOU KNOW ABOUT THE KING:

1 He has a rebellion on his hands but you don't know why.
2 The rebels include some of his best men, and are helped by Norwegian forces.
3 He is very surprised when he finds out about friends who turned against him.
4 He trusts Macbeth completely.
5 He promotes and honours those who help him very readily.
6 He is swift in judgement, quickly executing traitors and rebels.
7 He has two sons, the eldest of whom will be king after him.
8 The king himself does not fight, but leaves it to his generals.
9 He seems to be a mild and pleasant man in his behaviour.

- What do you like about this king?
- Why might you suspect that he is not a 'perfect' king?

FIG 4 Film still of a scene from *Far From the Madding Crowd*

the texture of the language so that pupils can still hear the quality of thought and feeling in the expression even if the structure and pace of the original are compromised.

In reality, teachers edit and abridge as they move through longer texts, by focusing on key passages and skipping over other stretches. It is not uncommon, for example, for teachers to edit out parts of Act 4 Scene 3 in *Macbeth* or Chapter One of *The Return of the Native*.

Whilst more able students can cope with the unabridged text, less confident readers can benefit from abridgement. However, there is no reason to buy special editions for less able readers if you specify which parts **must** be read. The benefit in working from the full text is that some will gain the confidence to read on, and the middle ability range will be realistically equipped to prioritise their reading if stamina fails.

Dividing the text

Some texts lend themselves to delegated study. They can be split up among students who then take responsibility for presenting them to the rest of the class.

Traditionally, teachers divide texts longitudinally. Short stories, in particular, can be divided into manageable sections with questions and activities interspersed throughout.

However, some texts lend themselves to division in another way so that separate groups can take one section and deal with it on behalf of the others, presenting their findings later. This strategy will only work with texts which do not depend on a single narrative sequence. Chaucer's *Prologue* is one example. Pupils might be grouped to consider the different characters; and in due course each will present a reading of its section, and an account of its findings

FIG 5 Sampling activity *Treasure Island*

You belong to a team of archaeologists who have discovered this chest containing what seem to be fragments of writing.

- Consider each piece of text and try to decide what they might mean.

Alexander Smollett, master; David Livesey, ship's doctor; Abraham Gray, carpenter's mate; John Trelawney, owner; John Hunter and Richard Joyce, owner's servants, landsmen – being all that is left faithful of the ship's company – with stores for ten days at short rations, came ashore this day, and flew British colours on the log-house in Treasure Island. Thomas Redruth, owner's servant, landsman, shot by the mutineers; James Hawkins, cabin boy –

'Fifteen men on the dead man's chest –
Yo-ho-ho, and a bottle of rum!
Drink and the devil had done for the rest –
Yo-ho-ho, and a bottle of rum!'

'Tall tree, Spy-glass shoulder, bearing a point to the N of NNE.
'Skeleton Island ESE and by E.
'Ten feet.
'The bar silver is in the north cache; you can find it by the trend of the east hummock, ten fathoms south of the black crag with the face on it.
'The arms are easy found, in the sand hill, N point of north inlet cape, bearing E, and a quarter N.

Old Anchor Inn, Bristol, March 1, 17–

'Dear Livesey. As I do not know whether you are at the Hall or still in London, I send this double to both places.

'The ship is bought and fitted. She lies at anchor, ready for sea. You never imagined a sweeter schooner – a child might sail her – two hundred tons; name, HISPANIOLA.

'I got her through my old friend, Blandly, who has proved himself throughout the most surprising trump. The admirable fellow literally slaved in my interest, and so, I may say, did everyone in Bristol, as soon as they got wind of the port we sailed for – treasure, I mean.'

for the rest of the class. In this way, everyone has access to the whole text but works closely on just one section. The example shown in Figure 6 shows how this can be organised in the classroom.

If the class is studying a poet such as Christina Rossetti, each small group may be given a different poem to explore. The class can then be jigsawed into new groups, each containing a representative of each of the original groups. Pupils then take turns to read and introduce their poem and findings to the new group. The new group can then discuss all they have heard and draw some conclusions about the poet and her work. The advantage of this method is that all pupils have to give feedback but no-one is put on the spot. The first group generates ideas and information, so that even the weakest pupil is armed with comments to take to their next group. They will be experts in their new group because no-one else will have encountered their poem before (see Figure 7).

Another way of using the 'jigsaw' is to allocate a single aspect of the text such as a character or theme to small groups of students who make notes as the text progresses and report back to the class periodically. Each group can be asked to make summary notes on one side of A4 to be distributed to the rest of the class once the text is finished.

Bridging devices

Teachers often speed up the reading of a longer text, moving between key passages and summarising elements of it which have been missed. Able students can be asked to perform this task.

Using a television or film adaptation is another possibility; teachers can move between priority passages, showing the intervening events on video and stopping short of the next passage. This is a sensible alternative to showing the whole film in advance of the reading. Students are sometimes disappointed when they move from the excitement of a blockbuster movie to the sedate Victorian novel which inspired it. On the other hand, it seems a waste to show it after the reading. Bridging is a respectable half-way function to help students through the text without spoiling their appetite.

Do remember that film-makers edit, and take liberties with the text. Students need to understand that film uses a different language: the grammar of cuts, fades, lighting, framing and angles. It is a different work of art, and not the same as a text constructed out of verbal language.

Taped readings

Taped readings can provide access to difficult texts for poor readers. A parent, support teacher or sixth former might be willing to read the priority passages onto tape if you publish a reading schedule. Tapes require concentration and a quiet place and time for listening. The library is a good venue, if the librarian has a copy of the reading schedule. If you purchase a pre-recorded tape, check

FIG 6 Chaucer's prologue

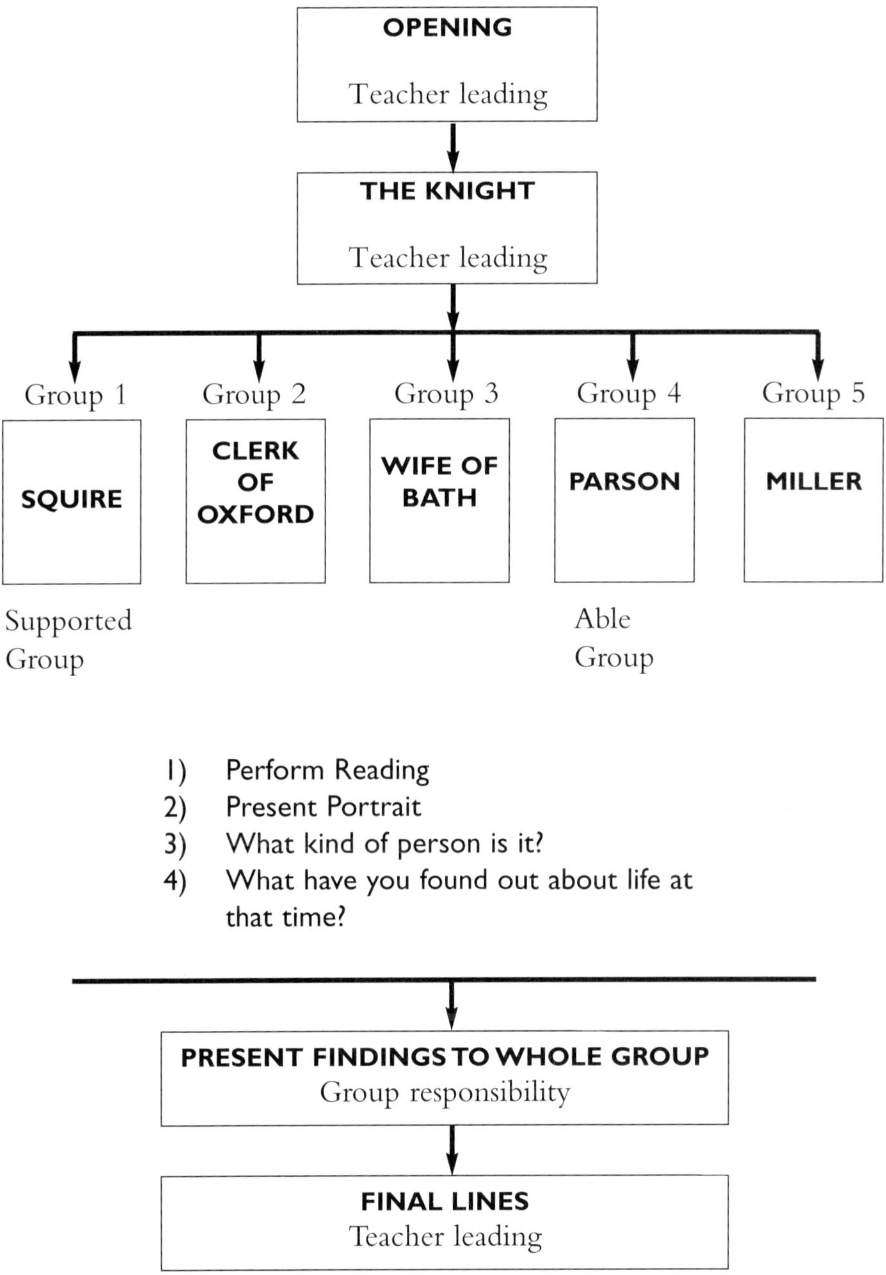

FIG 7 Dividing the text – Christina Rossetti's poetry

first that it is not abridged or simplified. Taped readings are especially useful when introducing students to Chaucer. Students will catch the meanings by listening to it far more effectively than if the text is treated as a foreign language to be translated on the page.

Keeping track

Students need to keep track of developing events, themes and characters as the text progresses, especially if they have to revise it for examination some months later. Detailed summaries are dull and time-consuming and students can buy them in study notes anyway. There are, however, some helpful alternatives, which involve students in periodic updating as they read.

FLOW CHART

What is it?

A flow chart lists the sequence of key events in the text to show cause-and-effect. Hence it may branch, link up or extend existing lines.

What do you do?

After each section of text, ask students to skim back over the text and update the line with key events.

Differentiation

- The more able can add on to the basic flow chart recording aspects of the novel's progress eg the development of characters or contrasts.
- The less able can be given prepared charts with some events already filled in, and identify the missing elements. Alternatively, cards with events written on them can be shuffled into order by referring to the text, and then added to the flow chart. It takes time to make cards like this, but they are a wonderful resource, and come in handy for revision.

What does it teach?

- It teaches students how to record the key events without writing reams of notes.
- It provides a quick résumé of the plot for revision.
- It sometimes clarifies the place, cause and significance of events in the plot.

Caution

There are no major pitfalls, except to keep an eye on the slow readers, and to give initial guidance about skimming.

FIG 8 Flow Chart – *Oliver Twist*

CHAPTER	EVENT
1	Oliver born in workhouse
	Mother dies
2	Moved to main workhouse by Mr Bumble
	Asks for more!
3	Solitary confinement
	Nearly becomes chimney sweep
4	Apprentice to undertakers
5	Attends death and funeral
6	Bullied by Noah
	Locked in cellar
7	Beaten by Bumble
	Runs away
8	Begging
	Found by Artful Dodger

TIME LINE

What is it?

A time line is a way of recording the key events of a plot against a time line, indicating the progress of fictional events in real time (see Figure 9).

What do you do?

After each section of text, ask students to skim over it and work out when the events happened in real time.

Differentiation

- The more able can be invited to tackle their time lines independently, commenting on the 'absent' time and why the writer has chosen to skip over it.
- The less able can be supported by giving a time line with relative times indicated and some key events already completed.

What does it teach?

This activity helps students to consider narrative structure and the time scale of the text. It is also an excellent vehicle for revision. The discussion of absent time in the novel can open out into a fruitful discussion of other absences – scenes, conversations and events which are not directly reported such as proposal scenes in the novels of Jane Austen or the life of Rochester after the fire in *Jane Eyre*.

Caution

The time line may be self-limiting since it tends to focus solely on key events.

TIME CHART

What is it?

A time chart is a structured way of recording the key events of the plot in diagrammatic form, as well as key characters and locations (see Figure 10).

What do you do?

After each major section of text, ask students to update the chart.

Differentiation

- The more able can be challenged to design their own time charts and to complete them independently.
- The less able can be supported by providing some of the entries on the chart and asking them to fill in the rest.

FIG 9 Time Line for *Jane Eyre*

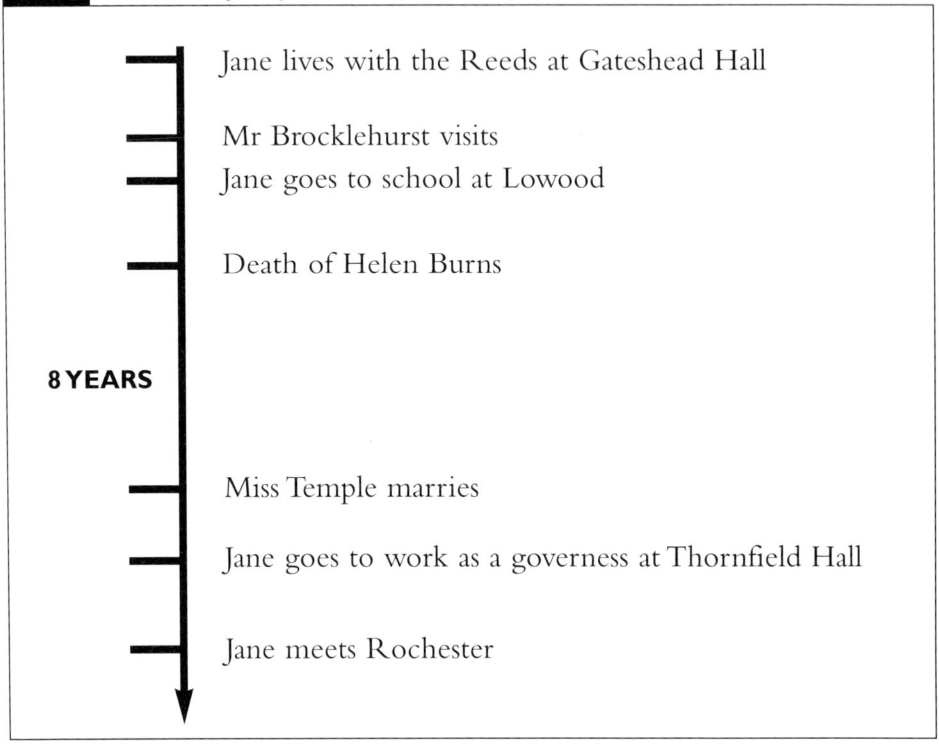

What does it teach?

- It enables the students to recognise and record the key events of the plot.
- It frees students from writing lengthy summaries, enabling them to chart relevant information such as the location of the chapter or the characters involved.

Caution

You need to devise headings which are pertinent to the text being studied. A general format may not suit every text.

READING JOURNAL

What is it?

A reading journal is a notebook in which students record their first, provisional responses to a text as they read it and monitor their developing attitudes and opinions. The journal is a private and personal document and therefore commonly happens inside the imagination written in note form. It is not for marking but for reading and occasionally responding. Its main function is to capture and clarify reading experiences at the time of reading.

FIG 10 Time Chart Grid for *Far from the Madding Crowd*

CHAPTER	TIME AND PLACE	CHARACTERS	KEY EVENTS
3	The shepherd's hut	Gabriel Oak Bathsheba Everdene	Bathsheba saves Oak's life
4	Bathsheba's aunt's cottage	Bathsheba Gabriel Oak Bathsheba's Aunt	Oak proposes to Bathsheba. She refuses him
5	Norcombe Hall The Chalk-pit	Gabriel Oak	Oak loses his sheep

What do you do?

Spend a lesson with students discussing what happens inside the imagination when we read. Give them the opening page to an accessible novel and ask them to jot down their fleeting impressions of the text. Invite them to feed their responses back to the class. Draw out from this feedback the active reading processes of, for example:

- making mental pictures
- anticipating the text
- questioning the text
- re-reading and relishing the text
- using one's own experience (personal or literary) to make sense of the text

As you launch the older text, give each student a notebook and ask them to record images, ideas, questions or impressions of the text at the time of reading. Suggest that they keep the journal by their side as they read and advise them that short, frequent responses are more helpful than long, retrospective ones.The journal is neither a plot summary nor a review - it is a place to capture emergent thinking about the text.

Allow time in the classroom, say three or four minutes at the end of the lesson, to make entries in the journal, and encourage students to do it at home as they read.

Begin to give prompts about how they might use them eg:'After reading this chapter, jot down in your journal any thoughts you have about changes in the character of Elizabeth/Jane' and draw on their entries in discussion.

If some students find it difficult to establish a style of writing in their journals, publish extracts to demonstrate the different approaches employed in the class. Ask permission first, as journals are personal documents. This can be helpful for those who have not yet found a comfortable voice. It is also a way of sharing reactions to the text.

What does it teach?

The journal stimulates the students to enter into an internal dialogue with themselves. Personal and fleeting impressions are externalised once articulated and the student can reflect and refine them. Research has also shown that students who have had time to note down their first responses are better able to contribute to group discussion. If students lapse into plot summary, they can be advised to record in question form only. The journal also has a practical function: here, students can fix factual aspects of a text such as names of characters or relationships between them.

As a teacher, the journals offer useful insights into the way your students are reading and allows you to direct and advise them as a result. Above all, it gives value and status to the students' personal responses which may not have been aired in a more public venue.

Caution

Some students express frustration that keeping the journal distracts them from reading. For some this is an excuse; for others it is true. Ironically, the value of the journal is that it does distract from immersion in the text, breaking a complacent reading habit. There is an intrusive element when the teacher reads a private journal: most students don't mind, but if it is an issue, it might be better to ask the student to keep the journal but not share it with you. Use reading journals sparingly or when you think it is necessary.

The opening chapters of a novel or the first encounters with a new poet are good examples of when to use a journal. At this time, novelists are trying hard to stimulate engagement, and students will be trying to sort out their first impressions.

Try keeping a journal yourself.

FIG 11 Reading Journal

Jane Eyre – Chapter One

Miserable setting in winter.
Miserable narrator – presumably Jane Eyre?
A lot about how cold, sad, raw it all is.

"She regretted to be under the necessity of keeping me at a distance" – did anyone ever speak like this? Sounds very formal.

— Can't work out who Bessie is.

"Shrined in double retirement" and so on. The language is dificult. Some bits are simple (eg how she was bullied) but the bits about conversations are hard to follow.

She fights back. But who is she? They are all called Reed and she is Eyre. A visitor? A cousin?

CHAPTER 3

Classroom approaches

EXPLORING THE LANGUAGE

Hands-on activities which invite students to sort, select, complete, annotate or restructure the text are particularly useful with older literature because they break down the inhibitions which students may have about unfamiliar language. More importantly, they encourage close reading and draw attention to specific aspects of the language. They elicit a positive, problem-solving attitude by enabling students to take ownership of the texts, thus de-mystifying them. What is more, students tend to enjoy them.

They do, however, have their drawbacks. For example, the materials cost time and money to produce, and there is a risk that students miss the point of doing them. The insights which can be gained from the activities have to be drawn out explicitly, and unless this happens, students treat them as a game and their teaching potential is lost.

SEQUENCING

What is it?

Students are asked to reassemble a piece of text, which has been arranged out of sequence.

What do you do?

Prior to the lesson, re-arrange the original text, eg re-order the stanzas of a poem or the paragraph of a story or the lines of a scene in a play. Ideally, you should copy these onto card, then cut up the lines. Laminate for durability. In the lesson, ask students, in pairs or groups, to reassemble the text. It helps if they are able to physically move the pieces around on the desk to try out different combinations. The final version can then be compared with the author's original.

Differentiation

- The more able can be challenged to draw out from their discussions what they have learnt about the structure of the text.
- The less able can be given some of the original text in sequence and asked to fit in others around them.

What does it teach?

Sequencing focuses attention on form and structure, such as narrative chronology, topic paragraphs or a rhyme scheme. It encourages students to think about the way in which a writer links, develops and extends ideas.

Caution

This activity works best in pairs or small groups; if you give it to individuals, they have nothing to challenge or improve their existing ideas. Sequencing works best if the teaching objective is to demonstrate plot, form or structure, so give careful thought to the 'break points' in the text. Segment the text so that reassembly will draw attention to the chosen aspect.

Examples

Figures 12 and 13 show sequencing activities on narrative poetry.

CLOZE PROCEDURE

What is it?

Cloze is text from which words have been systematically deleted and replaced with blanks.

What do you do?

Ask students, in groups, to speculate about the missing words and suggest possible replacements, finally fixing on the best proposal and filling it in. The finished cloze can then be compared with the author's original.

Differentiation

- The more able can be challenged to draw out from their discussions what they have learnt about the language chosen by the original author.
- The middle ability range can be supported by providing the deleted words in a list below the passage. Alternatively, they can be given the first letters.
- The less able are supported if groups are re-distributed after an initial discussion period, so that members compare answers in new groups. The least able bring to this new group ideas and suggestions culled from their original group.

What does it teach?

It focuses attention on vocabulary choices. In a chilling passage, the frightening words can be deleted. In a passage displaying bias, the biased words can be deleted. The effect of this is to draw attention to these words when the original is revealed.

Examples

- Figure 14 shows a simple cloze passage taken from *The Rainbow*. The words have been deleted to highlight the sensuousness of Lawrence's prose.
- Figure 15 shows a reverse cloze text from Gray's *Elegy*.

FIG 12 A sequencing activity on narrative poetry

An Elegy on the Death of a Mad Dog

The stanzas have been mixed up. Can you put them in the right order? What clues in the language help you to put them in the right order?

E

A kind and gentle heart he had,
To comfort friends and foes;
The naked every day he clad,
When he put on his clothes

A

The wound it seemed both sore and sad
To every Christian eye;
And while they swore the dog was mad,
They swore the man would die.

B

This dog and man at first were friends;
But when a pique began,
The dog, to gain his private ends,
Went mad, and bit the man.

C

Good people all, of every sort,
Give ear unto my song;
And if you find it wondrous short,
It cannot hold you long.

D

But soon a wonder came to light,
That showed the rogues they lied;
The man recovered of the bite,
The dog it was that died.

G

In Islington there was a man,
Of whom the world might say,
That still a godly race he ran,
Whene'er he went to pray.

H

Around from all the neighbouring streets
The wondering neighbours ran,
And swore the dog had lost his wits,
To bite so good a man.

F

And in that town a dog was found,
As many dogs there be,
Both mongrel, puppy, whelp, and hound,
And curs of low degree.

The correct order is: C, G, E, F, B, H, A, D.

FIG 13 Sequencing a sonnet

- Read this poem by Michael Drayton. The lines of the poem are not in their original order.
- Reassemble the poem. The first, fifth and ninth lines are indicated to help you.
- Check your version against the original.

a) Since there's no help, come let us kiss and part: (1st Line)
b) Nay, I have done; you get no more of me; (2nd Line)
c) And innocence is closing up his eyes;
d) Now, if thou would'st, when all have given him over,
e) From Death to Life thou might'st him yet recover.
f) And I am glad, yea, glad with all my heart
g) Be it not seen in either of our brows
h) When, his pulse failing, passion speechless lies,
i) That thus so cleanly I myself can free.
j) That we one jot of former love retain.
k) Now at the last gasp of love's latest breath (9th Line)
l) Shake hands forever; cancel all our vows; (5th Line)
m) When faith is kneeling by his bed of death
n) And when we meet at any time again,

DESCRIBE THE STRUCTURE OF THE POEM

You should consider:

- how many lines it has;
- how many syllables there are in each line;
- the rhythm of each line; and
- the rhyme scheme

Caution

Students sometimes treat cloze as a sort of test, and consider their answers 'wrong' if they are not used by the author. You have to explain that answers are neither right nor wrong, though some will be more apt than others. The author made certain choices, and it is both interesting and useful to recognise what is surprising, unusual or even predictable in them.

Reverse cloze is a variation on this activity in which students are presented with a list of words or phrases taken from a text and asked to speculate about them. A valuable spin-off from this activity is that pupils are made alert to those words and phrases when they eventually encounter them in the text.

COLOURING

What is it?

Colouring is when students use colour on a piece of text to suggest its emotional temperature, and to draw out the visual imagery.

What do you do?

Give the students a photocopy of the poem or passage and a set of colouring pencils. Ask them to colour over the words which refer to or suggest colours. Then ask them to broaden this by colouring over the emotional temperature of the lines.

Differentiation

- The more able can be challenged to explore the author's choice of language to suggest emotional intensity and the intended effect on the reader.
- The less able can be asked to look for particular emotions such as anger or sorrow. You can suggest obvious colours such as red or blue.

What does it teach?

This activity focuses attention on vocabulary choices, imagery and the sensual appeal of a text. This activity works particularly well with the *Odes* of Keats and the work of other Romantics. It also works well for descriptive and mood-setting descriptions. Hardy's landscapes are a good example. It highlights visual imagery, shifts of mood and appeals to the visual and emotional senses of the reader.

Caution

The text needs to be chosen carefully for its potential in terms of its imagery and emotional density. Some students may regard the exercise as non-literary.

FIG 14 A CLOZE worksheet on *The Rainbow* by D. H. Lawrence

The Rainbow – Worksheet

Read this passage from The Rainbow by D. H. Lawrence.

- Discuss which words would best fit the gaps.
- When you have finished, compare your choices with Lawrence's original.
- What do you find to confirm or surprise your expectations?
- Discuss Lawrence's choice of vocabulary and style.

But to him, she was a flame that ____________________ him. The ______________ flowed up his limbs, ________________ through him, till he was ____________________, till he existed only as an unconscious, dark transit of ___________________, deriving from her.

Sometimes in the _________________, a cow coughed. There was, in the darkness, a ______________ sound of cud chewing. And it all seemed to _______________ round them and upon them as the hot blood flows through the womb, laving the unborn ________________.

Sometimes, when it was cold, they stood to be ____________ in the stables, where the air was warm and ________________ with ammonia. And during these dark vigils, he learned _______________ know her, her body against his, they drew nearer ______________ nearer together, the kisses came more subtly close and __________________. So when in the thick darkness a horse suddenly _________________ to its feet, with a dull, thunderous sound, they _______________ as one person listening, they knew as one person, _________________ were conscious of the horse.

FIG 15 A reverse CLOZE worksheet on Gray's *Elegy*

Gray's Elegy – Worksheet

These words have been lifted – one from each two lines – from the poem you are about to study.

- What impression do you get of the poem's themes, style, setting, mood and age?

knell	lowly	moon
ploughman	blazing	grave
glimmering	return	forefathers
drowsy	sickle	pomp
yonder	jocund	rugged
ancient	ambition	grandeur

HIGHLIGHTING

What is it?

Highlighting is the practice of picking out related words and phrases in the text by underlining or highlighting. The words might be linked by theme, metaphor, argument, sound, function or other quality.

What do you do?

Give students a photocopy of the text and a selection of coloured highlighters. Explain the quality you are looking for in the words, eg words, suggestive of death, and locate the first example for them. Next, ask them to highlight all the other examples they can find in the text. If it is difficult to provide highlighter pens, the students can use a pen to underline, circle, box or bracket key words.

Differentiation

- The more able can be challenged to draw out from their discussions what they have learnt about the language chosen by the author and the effect on the reader.
- The less able can be supported by being given a text with some words already highlighted or given a specific number of words to find.

What does it teach?

Like cloze, highlighting focuses attention on vocabulary choices and draws explicit attention to the repetition, alliteration, leitmotiv and wordplay. In fact it is more flexible than cloze because it can be used to explore themes, characters and lines of argument.

Caution

Use sparingly. When students over-annotate a text it can be difficult for them to read the text with a fresh eye at a later date.

Examples

Figure 16 is an example of a text which could be used for highlighting - the highlighting could be used to reveal Juliet's inner conflict.

Figure 17 is a teacher's question sheet for the opening of *Bleak House*.

FIG 16 Juliet's speech – highlighting exercise

Juliet has to pluck up the courage to swallow the potion. What thoughts pass through her mind?

- In one colour, highlight the thoughts which persuade her to swallow the potion.
- In another colour, highlight the thoughts which make her hesitate.

I have a faint cold fear thrills through my veins
That almost freezes up the heat of life:
I'll call them back again to comfort me:
Nurse! – What should she do here?
My dismal scene I must needs act alone.
Come, vial.
What if this mixture do not work at all?
Shall I be married then tomorrow morning?
No, no, this shall forbid it; lie thou there.
[*Laying down her dagger*]
What if it be a poison which the friar
Subtly hath minister'd to have me dead,
Lest in this marriage he should be dishonoured,
Because he married me before to Romeo?
I fear it is; and yet, methinks, I should not,
For he hath still been tried a holy man.

FIG 17 *Bleak House* – highlighting worksheet

Bleak House

Read the following passage from *Bleak House* by Charles Dickens.

- Discuss the atmosphere which is created in this description. Find a word which sums it up e.g. Mysterious? Cold? Eerie?
- Underline or highlight all the words in the passage which help to create this atmosphere.
- In a different colour, highlight all the repeated nouns or phrases.
- Discuss what you have learnt about the language chosen by the author. What effect did it have on you as a reader?

'Fog everywhere. Fog up the river, where it flows among green aits and meadows; fog down the river, where it rolls defiled among the tiers of shipping, and the waterside pollution of a great (and dirty) city. Fog on the Essex Marshes; fog on the Kentish heights. Fog creeping into the cabooses of collier – brigs; fog lying out on the yards, and hovering in the rigging of great ships; fog drooping on the gunwales of barges and small boats. Fog in the eyes and throats of ancient Greenwich pensioners, wheezing by the firesides of their wards; fog in the stem and bowl of the afternoon pipe of the wrathful skipper, down in his close cabin; fog cruelly pinching the fingers and toes of his shivering little 'prentice boy on deck. Chance people on the bridges peeping over the parapets into a nether sky of fog, with fog all around them, as if they were up in a balloon, and hanging in the misty clouds.'

LINEATION

What is it?

Lineation is the practice of reconstructing a poem or even prose without the help of line breaks, punctuation or capital letters.

What do you do?

Type the text into the computer without line breaks or tell-tale capital letters. Then ask students to lay it out as they think it should be. Their version can then be compared with the poet's original.

Differentiation

- The more able can be extended by comparing their version with the original and discussing the reasons why the poet decided on particular line breaks and punctuation.
- The less able can be given extra help by being told how many lines there are in the original, or they may be given information about the structure.

What does it teach?

This activity focuses attention on poetic form and requires students to explore the poet's technique. It also prompts discussion about the difference between prose and poetry.

Caution

Students sometimes treat this activity as a kind of test and consider their version wrong if it does not match the original. You have to explain that their version is neither right nor wrong but that certain choices have been made for certain reasons which are worthy of discussion.

Example

Figure 18 shows *Pied Beauty* by Gerald Manley Hopkins. The poem has been typed without line breaks, punctuation or capital letters. Underneath it is the poet's original layout.

EDITING TO SPECIFICATION

What is it?

Editing to specification is the process of cutting a specific number of words or lines from a piece of text, for a given purpose or against particular priorities.

What do you do?

Give the students a poem or passage and ask them to edit it to, say, half its length. You may also ask them to do this in order to accentuate a particular theme, tone or point of view.

Differentiation

- The more able can be interrogated by the class and required to justify their reasons for editing out or leaving in certain words and phrases.
- The less able can be supported by being asked to edit a specific number of words from each line, verse or chunk of text.

What does it teach?

This activity requires students to consider what is important to the meaning,

FIG 18 *Pied Beauty* by G. M. Hopkins – lineation exercise

Pied Beauty
by G. M. Hopkins

Glory be to God for dappled things for skies of couple-colour as a brinded cow for rose-moles all in stipple upon trout that swim fresh-firecoal chestnut-falls finches' wings landscape plotted and pieced fold fallow and plough and all trades their gear and tackle and trim all things counter original spare strange whatever is fickle freckled (who knows how?) with swift slow sweet sour adazzle dim he fathers forth whose beauty is past change praise him.

- Read this poem which has been typed without punctuation, capital letters or line breaks.
- Decide where you would begin each new line.
- Decide where you would use punctuation and capital letters.
- Write out the poem, using punctuation, line breaks and capital letters.
- Compare your version with the poet's original.

THE ORIGINAL

Glory be to God for dappled things—
For skies of couple-colour as a brinded cow;
For rose-moles all in stipple upon trout that swim;
Fresh-firecoal chestnut-falls finches' wings;
Landscape plotted and pieced—fold fallow and plough;
And all trades their gear and tackle and trim.

All things counter, original spare, strange;
Whatever is fickle, freckled (who knows how?)
With swift, slow; sweet, sour; adazzle, dim:
He fathers-forth whose beauty is past change:
Praise him.

and what is lost if detail or description is ignored. All writers prune their work, but this drafting process is virtually always invisible to the reader. The activity throws a dramatic light on the core meaning of the text.

Caution

Some students do not enjoy editing what they may see as a sacrosanct text. It is helpful if a context for the exercise can be provided such as limited column space in a magazine, the drafting process or an understanding of the editorial role.

Example

Figure 19 shows a teacher's worksheet for *At Castle Boterel* by Thomas Hardy and one group's answer.

TRANSPOSITION

What is it?

Transposition or textual re-casting is the conversion of one piece of text into a different literary format.

What do you do?

Give the students a piece of text and ask them to convert it into another, and then compare them.

Differentiation

- The more able can be extended by asking them to generalise about the characteristics of different literary forms.
- The less able can be supported by being given a framework for the new text eg a play script which includes the names of the characters and where they speak.

What does it teach?

This activity helps students to consider what is lost and gained in different literary formats. It also enhances their own competence as writers.

Caution

Students need to know how to write a play script or whatever format they have been asked to use. Some teaching time needs to be set aside for this.

Example

Figure 20 shows a transposition activity using *Jane Eyre*.

FIG 19 *At Castle Boterel* by Thomas Hardy – editing to specification

At Castle Boterel by Thomas Hardy

- Read this poem by Thomas Hardy. Your task is to edit the poem to approximately half its original length whilst retaining its meaning.
- Write out your edited version.
- Compare your version with the original. Discuss what has been lost and gained.

AT CASTLE BOTEREL (ORIGINAL VERSION)

As I drive to the junction of lane and highway,
And the drizzle bedrenches the waggonette,
I look behind at the fading byway,
And see on its slope, now glistening wet,
Distinctly yet

Myself and a girlish form benighted
In dry March weather. We climb the road
Beside a chaise. We have just alighted
To ease the sturdy pony's load
When he sighed and slowed.

What we did as we climbed, and what we talked of
Matters not much, nor to what it led,—
Something that life will not be balked of
Without rude reason till hope is dead,
And feeling fled.

It filled but a minute. But was there ever
A time of such quality, since or before,
In that hill's story? To one mind never,
Though it has been climbed, foot swift, foot-sore,
By thousands more.

Primaeval rocks form the road's steep border,
And much have they faced there, first and last,
Of the transitory in Earth's long order;
But what they record in colour and cast
Is—that we two passed.

FIG 19 *At Castle Boterel* by Thomas Hardy – editing to specification

And to me, though Time's unflinching rigour,
In mindless rote, has ruled from sight
The substance now, one phantom figure
Remains on the slope, as when that night
Saw us alight.

I look and see it there, shrinking, shrinking,
I look back at it amid the rain
For the very last time; for my sand is sinking,
And I shall traverse old love's domain
Never again.

• •

AT CASTLE BOTEREL (EDITED VERSION)

As I drive to the junction of lane and highway,
And the drizzle bedrenches the waggonette,
I look behind, and see
Myself and a girlish form
In dry March weather.

We climb the road beside a chaise.
What we did, and what we talked of
Matters not much.
It filled but a minute
But was there ever
A time of such quality
In that hill's story?

Though it has been climbed by thousands more,
Primaeval rocks form the road's border
But what they record is—
that we two passed.

One phantom figure remains.
I look and see it shrinking amid the rain.
I shall traverse love's domain
Never again.

FIG 20 Transposition exercise on *Jane Eyre*

Discuss how you might turn the opening chapter of Jane Eyre into a script for radio.

- What would you need to add, omit or change?
- Consider the use of music, sound effects (SFX) and voice overs (VO)
- Write the opening in script form.

NOTES:

SCRIPT:

***SFX** Soft, classical music which fades*

VO (*Jane*): I had been banished from the company of my aunt for the afternoon. Until she heard from Bessie that I was able to adopt a more sociable and childlike disposition she really must exclude me from privileges.... I didn't mind. I had retreated to the window seat with my book – Bewick's History of British Birds – to escape from my cousins. I was happy; happy at least in my way....

***SFX** Door bangs open*

John Where the Dickens is she! Lizzy! Georgy! Joan is not here. Tell Mama.

Eliza She is in the window-seat, to be sure Jack

***SFX** A cry, indicating pain*

Approaching text through performance

We are prone to think of reading as a private and intensely personal experience but this is not the way texts were habitually read over the centuries, nor the way writers imagined their readers. It is only relatively recently that mass literacy and the efficient printing press have made it possible to privatise reading. Before the twentieth century, society was organised for mass illiteracy which was ideal for the cultivation of an oral culture. Stories, poems and songs were passed on by word of mouth and drama was written to be received by ear and eye. The first poems were lyrics to be sung as part of a musical entertainment. During the nineteenth century, novels were often read aloud among families, and are easier to read aloud than one might expect.

RECITATION

What do you do?

Divide a poem into very short sections - perhaps one or two lines. Allocate sections to students in the class and ask them to read their lines aloud at the appropriate time so that the class delivers the poem in its entirety. Then ask students to memorise their lines. Allow them time to practise. Ask them to deliver their lines again, this time without the constraints of the text in front of them.

Examples

- The dramatic monologues of Robert Browning
- *John Gilpin* by William Cowper
- *Reynard the Fox* by John Masefield

Why do it?

Older prose lends itself surprisingly well to recitation and oral delivery. Victorian punctuation is particularly helpful in this respect. Dickens, for example, was a celebrated reader of his own texts. Fee-paying audiences wept and fainted when he read aloud the death of Nancy in *Oliver Twist*. As an alternative, there are professional artists who will perform extracts from Dickens and Chaucer for groups of students.

SOUND EFFECTS

What do you do?

Divide the class into groups and give each group a poem or passage. Ask them to underline references to sound and atmosphere. Then ask them to read poetry or passages into a tape recorder. Invite them to add simple but appropriate sound effects.

Examples

- Mimetic poems such as Robert Louis Stevenson's *From a Railway Carriage* or Tennyson's *The Charge of the Light Brigade*
- *The Highwayman* by Alfred Noyes
- *Morte d'Arthur* by Tennyson

Why do it?

Students who find the threat of live performance daunting will feel more secure using a tape recorder. The text can be brought to life off the page in an imaginative but unintimidating way.

SNIPPETS

What do you do?

Clear a space. Place a number of sheets around the floor, each one containing a telling line from the text. Ask students to wander round, reading out aloud the snippets as they come upon them (see Figure 21).

Examples

- Snippets from Lady Macbeth's sleepwalking scene
- Phrases from *The Highwayman*
- Insults from *Romeo and Juliet*
- Descriptive details of key characters in a Dickens novel

Why do it?

Using this activity to introduce a text engages the students' curiosity and gives them a feel for the language. It encourages students to speculate about the context and what led the characters to this situation. Students then greet the text with some degree of familiarity, confidence and enthusiasm. There is no particular need to begin a text at the beginning.

You can also use this activity to introduce a topic of discussion such as Dickens' pen portraits or the feud in *Romeo and Juliet*. It is a lively and positive way of getting students to pay close attention to language.

IMPROVISATION WITH CUES

What do you do?

Organise students into groups and give them a tantalising extract from a key scene so that they understand the context. Ask them to improvise this scene, and also the events leading up to it and after it.

Examples

- The sleepwalking scene in *Macbeth*

FIG 21 Sleepwalking scene from *Macbeth* – snippets exercise

Sleepwalking Snippets

'What a sigh is there!'

'Yet here's a spot.'

'Out damned spot.'

'So much blood in him.'

'There's the smell of the blood still.'

'A soldier and afeard?'

'What's done cannot be undone.'

'There's knocking at the gate.'

'Look, how she rubs her hands.'

'Hell is murky.'

- The wife-selling scene in *The Mayor of Casterbridge* (see Figure 22)
- Elizabeth's rejection of Darcy's proposal in *Pride and Prejudice*
- Romeo at Juliet's tomb
- The ghost of Banquo at the banquet in *Macbeth*

Why do it?

This activity makes a dramatic start to the study of the text by entering it at a pivotal moment. It arouses students' curiosity and acquaints them with the language and the plot. It has a considerable impact on their reading of the text because they know where some of the events are leading, and they are primed to watch out for signs of what is to come. It can be useful with classes who have not pre-read the text, and also with texts that have a slow opening.

STRIDING THE SPEECH

What do you do?

Use a soliloquy the first time you try this. Choose one person to read, but at each punctuation mark, ask the student to stride five paces, stop and read up to the next mark, then stride five paces back and so on. They can then be asked where the power of the speech lies, and what are its most moving and dramatic moments.

A variation on this activity is to seat the class in a circle and ask them to read around the group, reading slowly and handing over to their neighbour at the next punctuation mark.

Another variation is to put students into groups, taking turns to 'stride' and observe each other.

Examples

- Any soliloquy or 'big speech' from Shakespeare (see Figure 23)
- Lyrical or descriptive poetry, especially Wordsworth, Keats and Gray
- Some reflective passages in Hardy's novels.

Why do it?

The speech is broken down into manageable chunks, giving full force to each phrase. The reader hangs upon the next section and catches the full emotional force of the speech by reliving it in slow motion. Individual phrases are noticed. Students acquire a heightened sense of the rhythm, expression and dramatic impact of the passage.

CHORAL PERFORMANCE

What do you do?

Organise students into groups to prepare a reading for several voices. This

FIG 22 Improvisation exercise on *The Mayor of Casterbridge*

The Mayor of Casterbridge

'Mike, Mike,' said she; 'this is getting serious. O! – too serious!'

'Will anybody buy her?' said the man.

'I wish somebody would,' said she firmly. 'Her present owner is not at all to her liking!'

'Nor you to mine,' said he. 'So we are agreed about that. Gentlemen, you hear? It's an agreement to part. She shall take the girl if she wants to, and go her ways. I'll take my tools, and go my ways. 'Tis simple as Scripture history. Now then, stand up, Susan, and show yourself.'

'Don't, my chiel,' whispered a buxom staylace dealer in voluminous petticoats, who sat near the woman; 'yer good man don't know what he's saying.'

The woman, however, did stand up. 'Now, who's auctioneer?' cried the hay-trusser.

'I be,' promptly answered a short man, with a nose resembling a copper knob, a damp voice, and eyes like button-holes. 'Who'll make an offer for this lady?'

The woman looked on the ground, as if she maintained her position by a supreme effort of will.

'Five shillings,' said some one, at which there was a laugh.

'No insults,' said the husband. 'Who'll say a guinea?'

Nobody answered; and the female dealer in staylaces interposed.

'Behave yerself moral, good man, for Heaven's love! Ah, what a cruelty is the poor soul married to ! Bed and board is dear at some figures, 'pon my 'vation 'tis!'

'Set it higher, auctioneer,' said the trusser.

'Two guineas!' said the auctioneer; and no one replied.

'If they don't take her for that, in ten seconds they'll have to give more,' said the husband. 'Very well. Now auctioneer, add another.'

'Three guineas – going for three guineas!' said the rheumy man.

'No bid?' said the husband. 'Good Lord, why she's cost me fifty times the money, if a penny. Go on.'

'Four guineas!' cried the auctioneer.

'I'll tell ye what – I won't sell her for less than five,' said the husband, bringing down his fist so that the basins danced. 'I'll sell her for five guineas to any man that will pay me the money, and treat her well; and he shall have her for ever, and never hear aught o' me. But she shan't go for less. Now then – five guineas – and she's yours. Susan, you agree?'

FIG 22 Improvisation exercise on *The Mayor of Casterbridge*

Questions about the passage

- Read the passage and discuss what you think is happening in this scene in your group.
- Act out the scene in your group.
- Work out what led up to it and try acting this out too.
- Discuss what may happen next.
- This scene comes from the opening of our new text, *The Mayor of Casterbridge*. What is most likely to happen given that this is just the first chapter?

could be a choral effort or a reading for different voices working together. It is helpful to appoint a director for each group and to offer a tape recorder if a live performance is daunting. Students can use a variety of tactics:

- Soft echoes of key words
- Choral reading
- Voices which join at certain points
- Voices which take over for certain lines
- Sound effects or music

Examples

- Dramatic passages from *Beowulf*
- Juliet's soliloquy in which she debates drinking the potion
- Atmospheric or confessional poems
- The cauldron chant from *Macbeth* (see Figure 24)

Why do it?

This activity familiarises students with the language and prepares them for reading aloud a part later in the play. It capitalises on the oral quality of dramatic rhyme. The process can also throw new light on the passage. Juliet's soliloquy, for example, is revealed as an inner dialogue. This activity builds confidence and students enjoy it.

FIG 23 'Striding the speech' exercise – Hamlet's soliogury

Hamlet

IN YOUR GROUP

- Sit in a circle.
- Read the text slowly until you reach a mark. When you reach a mark, the person to your left should continue and so on.
- Choose a reader to stand up. Read to the first mark and then stride five paces. Read to the next mark and stride back five paces. This will leave gaping of silence at each punctuation mark. Continue like this until you have read the whole speech.

HAMLET'S SOLILOQUY

To be / or not to be / that is the question: /
Whether 'tis nobler in the mind to suffer
The slings and arrows of outrageous fortune /
Or to take arms against a sea of troubles /
And by opposing end them? / To die / to sleep /
No more / and by a sleep to say we end
The heartache / and the thousand natural shocks
That flesh is heir to / 'Tis a consummation
Devoutly to be wish'd / To die / to sleep /
To sleep / perchance to dream / ay / there's the rub /
When we have shuffled off this mortal coil /
Must give us pause / There's the respect /
That makes calamity of so long life

- Discuss what you noticed about the speech when you read it like this.
- Where does its power lie?
- What insights does it give us into Hamlet's state of mind?

FIG 24 Choral performance exercise from *Macbeth*

- Work in groups of three and allocate parts.
- Practise reading your parts. You should read the lines for 'All' together.
- Try different ways of reading the lines – loudly, softly, etc.
- Discuss what you notice about the language, and write down some words to describe it.

THE CAULDRON CHANT (FROM MACBETH)

First Witch: Round about the cauldron go;
In the poison'd entrails throw.
Toad, that under cold stone
Days and nights has thirty-one
Swelter'd venom sleeping got,
Boil thou first i' the charmed pot.

All: Double, double, toil and trouble;
Fire burn and cauldron bubble.

Second Witch: Fillet of a fenny snake,
In the cauldron boil and bake;
Eye of newt and toe of frog,
Wool of bat and tongue of dog,
Adder's fork and blind-worm's sting,
Lizard's leg and howlet's wing,
For a charm of powerful trouble,
Like a hell-broth boil and bubble.

All: Double, double, toil and trouble;
Fire burn and cauldron bubble.

Third Witch: Scale of dragon, tooth of wolf,
Witches' mummy, maw and gulf
Of the ravin'd salt-sea shark,
Root of hemlock digg'd i' the dark,
Liver of blaspheming Jew,
Gall of goat, and slips of yew
Silver'd in the moon's eclipse,
Nose of Turk and Tartar's lips,
Finger of birth-strangled babe
Ditch-deliver'd by a drab,
Make the gruel thick and slab:
Add thereto a tiger's chaudron,
For the ingredients of our cauldron.

All: Double, double, toil and trouble;
Fire burn and cauldron bubble.

Second Witch: Cool it with a baboon's blood,
Then the charm is firm and good.

FREEZE FRAMES

What do you do?

Choose a key point in the text particularly one which features a critical moment in the relationships between characters. Organise students into groups, and ask each student to take a different character in the scene. Next, ask them to move into position to create a tableau or freeze frame of the moment in the text. In other words, they use themselves to model the still image. Once the groups are ready, allow time for each group to come out of role to look at the other groups. You can extend this activity by asking characters to speak aloud their thoughts and feelings at this dramatic moment by asking, 'Tell us what you are thinking right now, as your character?'

Example

- St John Rivers' proposal to Jane Eyre
- Troy's return at the New Year's Eve party in *Far From The Madding Crowd*
- The four characters in *Cousin Kate* by Christina Rossetti

Why do it?

This activity requires students to climb into the skin of the characters at a pivotal moment in the text. It enables them to consider motive and relationships and throws a new light on silent and minor characters. It takes a little time, but students resume their reading with greater understanding and empathy.

ECHOING

What do you do?

Choose a scene from the text which involves an argument or conflict between characters. Allocate the key parts and ask them to stand facing each other if there are two, or in a triangle as three, etc. Provide each one with a small group of supporters to stand just behind them. The role of the supporters is to echo key words during the reading.

Examples

- The conflict between Oberon and Titania in *A Midsummer Night's Dream* (see Figure 26)
- The desperate pleas of Fanny to Troy after missing the wedding in *Far From The Madding Crowd*
- Macbeth and Lady Macbeth discussing whether to proceed with the murder
- Nancy pleading for her life to Bill Sykes

FIG 25 Freeze frame activity

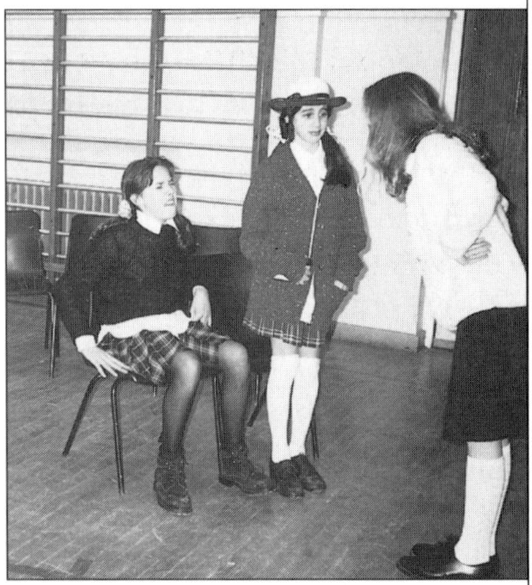

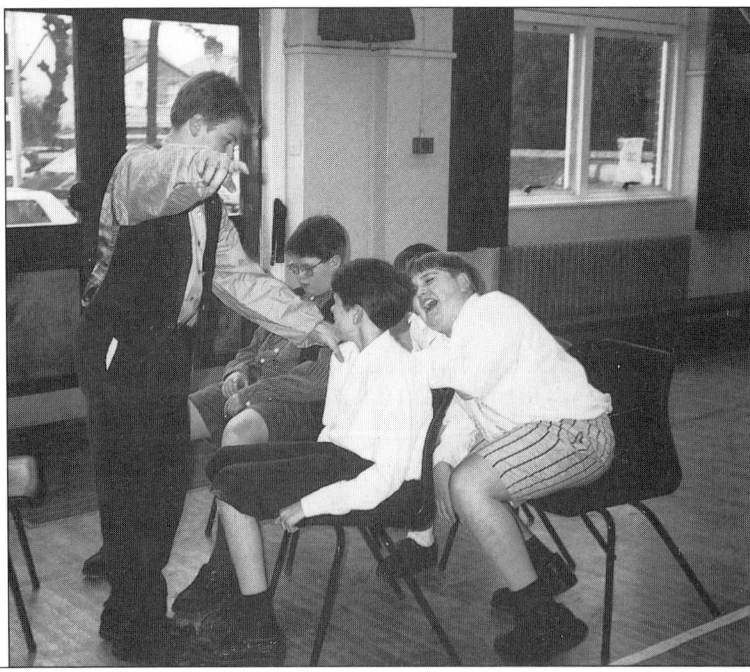

FIG 26 Echoing activity from *A Midsummer Night's Dream*

A Midsummer Night's Dream

- Rehearse the passage first.
- Titania and Oberon face each other and act out the argument.
- Supporters crowd behind and echo key phrases. (The first few have been highlighted for you)

EXCERPT FROM A MIDSUMMER NIGHT'S DREAM

Oberon Ill met by moonlight, **proud Titania**

Titania What, **jealous Oberon**! Fairies, skip hence.
I have **forsworn** his bed and company.

Oberon Tarry, **rash wanton**, am not I thy **lord**?

Titania Then I must be **thy lady**: but I know
When thou hast **stolen away** from fairy land
And in the shape of Corin sat all day,
Playing on pipes of corn, and versing **love**
To amorous **Phillida**. Why art thou **here**,
Come from the farthest steppe of **India**?
But that, forsooth, the bouncing Amazon,
Your buskin'd mistress and your warrior love,
To Theseus must be wedded, and you come
To give their bed joy and prosperity.

Oberon How canst thou thus for shame, Titania,
Glance at my credit with Hippolyta,
Knowing I know thy love to Theseus?
Didst thou not lead him through the glimmering night
From Perigenia, whom he ravished?
And make him with fair Aegle break his faith,
With Ariadne and Antiopa?

Titania These are the forgeries of jealousy:
And never, since the middle summer's spring,
Met we on hill, in dale, forest, or mead,
By paved fountain or by rushy brook,
Or in the beached margent of the sea,
To dance our ringlets to the whistling wind,
But with thy brawls thou hast disturbed our sport.

Oberon Why should Titania cross her Oberon?
I do but beg a little changeling boy,
To be my henchman.

FIG 26 Echoing activity from *A Midsummer Night's Dream*

Titania Set your heart at rest,
The fairy land buys not the child of me.
His mother was a votaress of my order,
But she, being mortal, of that boy did die;
And for her sake do I rear up her boy,
And for her sake I will not part with him.

Oberon Give me that boy, and I will go with thee.

Titania Not for thy fairy kingdom. Fairies, away!
We shall chide downright, if I longer stay.

Oberon Well, go thy way. Thou shalt not from this grove
Till I torment thee for this injury.

Why do it?

This activity highlights vocabulary choices and the emotional charge of dialogue. The sense of conflict is heightened and students are more easily able to see the development of the argument. Readers are supported by class members who are all actively engaged in the activity.

HOT SEATING

What do you do?

Choose a confident student and ask him or her to go into role as a character in the text. The rest of the class may now ask questions of the character about their actions, motives and views. The activity works best when students are seated in a close circle around a chair where the interviewee is placed.

Examples

- Fagin in *Oliver Twist*
- Friar Lawrence in *Romeo and Juliet*
- The lady in *La Belle Dame Sans Merci*
- Mrs Pearce in *Pygmalion*

FIG 27 Hotseating exercise

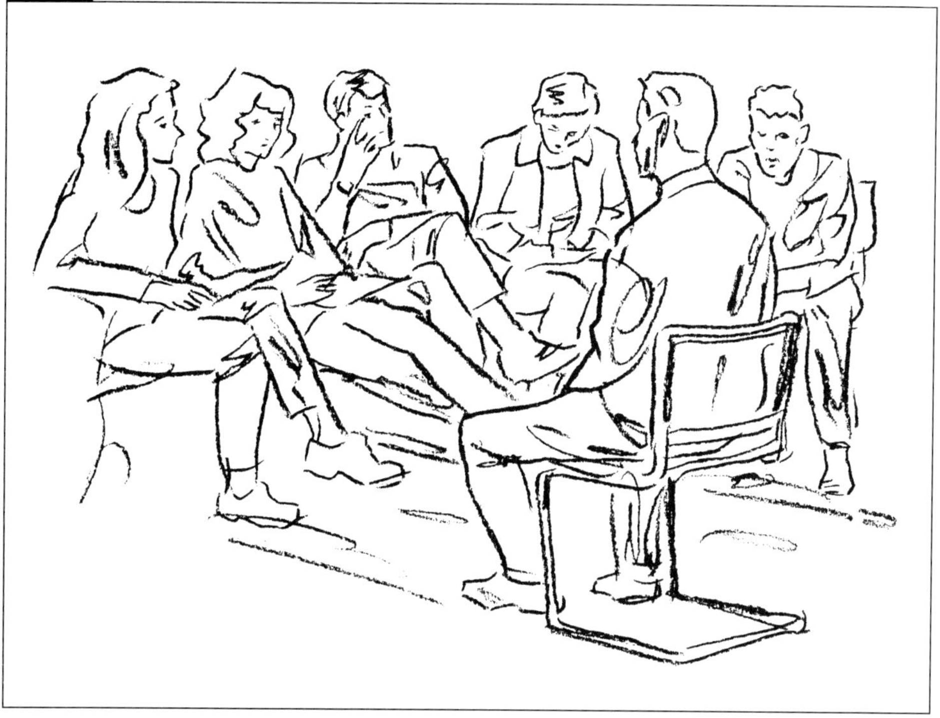

Why do it?

This is a very challenging activity for the student in role and a good way of stretching able students. You can encourage others to participate by organising the activity in groups, with each group hotseating a different character. Tricky questions can be discussed in the groups so that the interviewee is well rehearsed when the interview is replayed for the rest of the class. Another approach is to issue the questions in advance, so that interviewees have time to prepare their answers.

ANNOTATION FOR PERFORMANCE

What do you do?

Explain to students that they are going to direct a group of actors to perform a particular scene from the set play. However, they will not be there to talk the actors through it, so it must be done in writing. They will need to block movements and make notes for the actors. You might give them a specific brief by asking them, for example, to bring out the humour or show the relationship between two characters.

FIG 28 Annotated scene from *Macbeth*

ACT V.

SCENE I. *Dunsinane. Ante-room in the castle.*

Enter a Doctor of Physic *and* a Waiting-Gentlewoman.

Doct. I have two nights watched with you, but can perceive no truth in your report. When was it she last walked?

Gent. Since his majesty went into the field, I have seen her rise from her bed, throw her night-gown upon her, unlock her closet, take forth paper, fold it, write upon't, read it, afterwards seal it, and again return to bed; yet all this while in a most fast sleep.

Doct. A great perturbation in nature, to receive at once the benefit of sleep, and do the effects of watching! In this slumbery agitation, besides her walking and other actual performances, what at any time, have you heard her say?

Gent. That, sir, which I will not report after her.

Doct. You may to me: and 'tis most meet you should.

Gent. Neither to you nor any one; having no witness to confirm my speech.

Enter LADY MACBETH, with a taper.

Lo you, here she comes! This is her very guise; and, upon my life, fast asleep. Observe her; stand close.

Doct. How came she by that light?

Gent. Why, it stood by her; she has light by her continually; 'tis her command.

Doct. You see, her eyes are open.

Gent. Ay, but their sense is shut.

Doct. What is it she does now? Look, how she rubs her hands.

Gent. It is an accustomed action with her, to seem thus washing her hands: I have known her continue in this a quarter of an hour.

Lady M. Yet here's a spot.

Doct. Hark! she speaks: I will set down what comes from her, to satisfy my remembrance the more strongly.

Lady M. Out, damned spot! out I say!—One: two: why, then 'tis time to do't.—Hell is murky!—Fie, my lord, fie! a soldier, and afeard? What need we fear who knows it, when none can call our power to account?—Yet who would have thought the old man to have had so much blood in him?

- Enters on raised dias centre, back (a)
- By candlelight
- Carrying candle
- Doctor carrying medicine bag
- Stage whisper, gradually increasing in volume
- Moves forward to (b)
- Moves towards doctor
- Looks towards L.M. – Moves back to (a)
- Entrance (D) – moves swiftly forward towards (c), sits and puts candle on table
- Doctor points to L.M.
- Holds hands up in front of her face
- Doctor writes on note-paper
- Moves to (e) with candle
- Shakes her head
- Raises hands in air, gasps for breath
- Looks into candle on the word 'blood.' Guards candle with her hand.

Example

- Key scenes from Shakespeare (see Figure 28)

Why do it?

This activity requires close reading and encourages students to consider the dramatic possibilities of play scripts. It provides an active, hands-on approach which allows the students to take ownership of the text. Above all, it enables students to understand that different interpretations are not only possible but desirable.

GROUP PERFORMANCE

What is it?

Groups of students are allocated a section of the set play to study and perform (see Figure 29). This activity works particularly well with a play in which the language is reasonably accessible.

Start by explaining the plot of the play, and allow the groups to rehearse and perform their sections. Try giving the groups an added brief eg concentrate on the humour or bring out the relationships between characters. It is useful to video performances such as these for closer and more critical study later on.

FIG 29 Students in performance

Examples
- *She Stoops to Conquer* by Goldsmith
- *Pygmalion* by Shaw.

Why do it?
Students are able to regard the play script as a piece of drama which is brought to life through performance. They can be encouraged to consider different possibilities of interpretations as well as exploring theatrical aspects such as blocking, costume and lighting if desired.

Picturing the past

The world of Dickens or Austen resembles only in part the world with which our students are acquainted, so part of teaching older literature will involve familiarising students with the historical context of the work. We should not be over anxious; the text itself is a good introduction to the past because it immerses the students in the imaginative experience of being there. The writers of bygone cultures reveal themselves in the fabric of their telling; from their imaginings the reader can reconstruct their values, preoccupations and ideals and something of their circumstances.

MATCHING TEXT AND ILLUSTRATION

What do you do?
Long narrative poems such as Coleridge's *The Rime of the Ancient Mariner*, Tennyson's *The Lady of Shalott* and Noyes' *The Highwayman* have all been published in superbly illustrated editions. A list of recommendations can be seen on pp. 73–74. Give students a set of the illustrations and a separate set of pages of written text. One way of doing this without breaching copyright laws is by carefully dismantling a book. Ask students to match the text to the illustrations.

Why do it?
Illustrated editions of older texts can provide information about a text's historical, social and cultural context at a glance. Thoughtful illustrations will stimulate the reader and are especially supportive for the least able readers who are able to take their cues from the pictures. Some of the very best illustrations cast an intriguing light on the text and are worthy of attention in their own right (see Figures 30 and 31).

FIG 30 An illustration by Charles Keeping from *Beowulf*

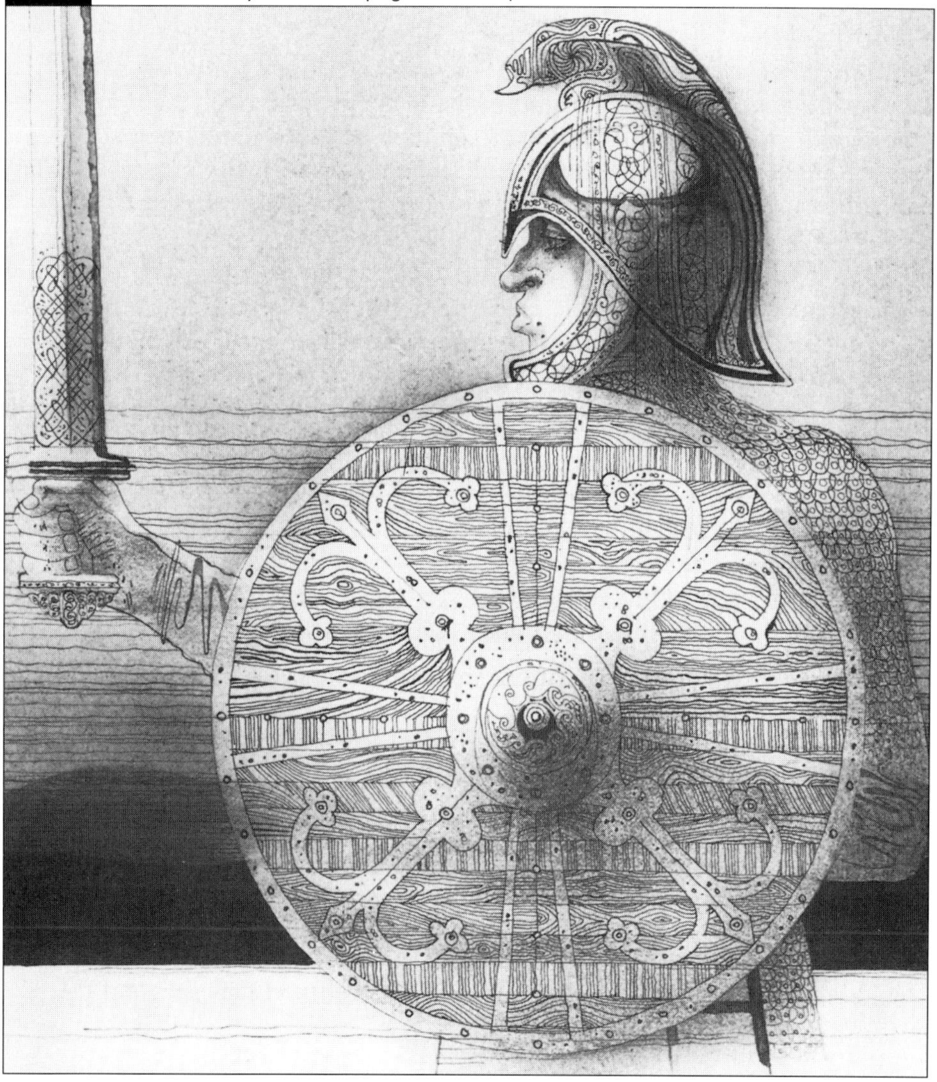

SEQUENCING ILLUSTRATIONS

What do you do?

Prior to reading a long narrative poem such as Coleridge's *The Rime of the Ancient Mariner*, give students a set of the illustrations and ask them to sequence them to tell a story. Students can then be asked to tell their stories to the class. Once the poem has been read, students can be invited to explore the similarities and differences between their version and the poet's own.

Why do it?

As a pre-reading activity, less able readers are given the confidence to progress to a more detailed study of the poem through familiarity with the plot. The activity works equally well with illustrations from a novel such as *Treasure Island* by Robert Louis Stevenson, *Gulliver's Travels* by Swift or *Alice in Wonderland* by Lewis Carroll.

CONTRASTING IMAGES

What do you do?

Find contrasting images such as different paintings of *The Lady of Shalott*. Divide the class into groups. Give each group one of the paintings. Ask them to analyse the images through a series of simple questions such as:

- who is the lady?
- what is she doing?
- where is she?

Example

Why do it?

This activity can be used as a pre-reading activity to give students confidence to approach the text with a greater degree of familiarity. It can also be used once the text has been studied to stimulate discussion about different interpretations of the text.

SKETCHING ACTIVITIES

What do you do?

Older writers are often lavish in their description of people and places. Since they were writing at a time before the photograph or lithograph, they relied on vivid writing to create images.

FIG 31 Illustrations of *The Rime of the Ancient Mariner* by Gustave Dore

Example

Ask students to sketch any of the following:

- a setting or stage plan from information provided by the author, for example the red room in *Jane Eyre* or George Bernard Shaw's description of the stage set in *Pygmalion* (see Figure 34);
- recurring key images such as night time images in *Macbeth*, images of cold in *The Rime of the Ancient Mariner* or images of air, rock, fire and water in *Jane Eyre*;
- a family tree as the reader is introduced to new characters in the book, for example, Jane Eyre's family tree or the Bennet family tree in *Pride and Prejudice*;
- a character from a set text using the author's description as guidance, for example, Defoe's detailed pen portrait of *Robinson Crusoe* or Benn Gunn in *Treasure Island* (see Figures 35 and 36);
- a new book jacket for a novel, designed to highlight particular aspects of a text and lure potential readers.

FIG 34 Sketch from *The Woodlanders* (pupil work)

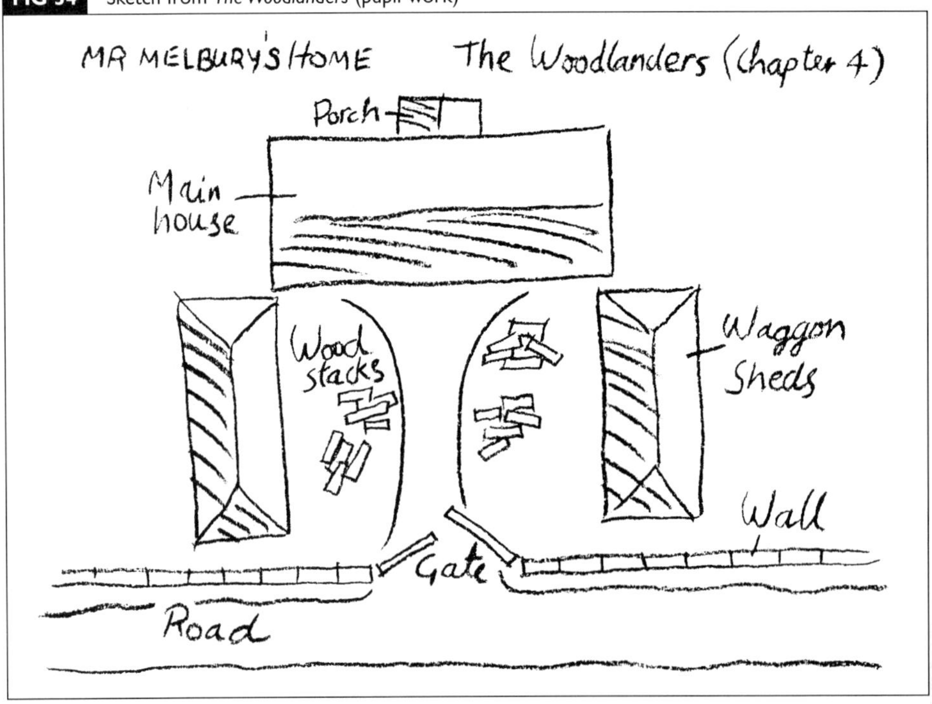

FIG 35 Sketch of Robinson Crusoe (pupil work)

FIG 36 Sketch by pupil – Jim meets Ben Gunn

Why do it?

Sketching activities help readers to make mental pictures of aspects of the text as they read. They help students to visualise the world of the text in a creative way which is still firmly rooted in the language. Students who lack artistic skills can be asked to draw up instructions for an illustrator based on textual information and personal interpretation, such as the contents of the chest in *Treasure Island* or the wedding banquet in *Great Expectations*.

RESEARCHING THE HISTORICAL CONTEXT

There are many other ways of providing access to the world of the text for students to whom it will be all too unfamiliar. Here are a few of them:

Visits to literary shrines

Obvious examples include Rochester (Dickens), Stratford (Shakespeare), Chawton (Jane Austen), Haworth (the Brontës), Canterbury (Chaucer), Hampstead (Keats) and Dorchester (Hardy). Build into your outing a visit to settings described in novels and study them in situ, for example Hardy's Wessex or the inspiration for *Wuthering Heights* near Haworth.

Research assignments

- Split the class into groups to research different historical aspects, such as:
  - Publication - serialisation, pseudonyms, drafting process.
  - Contemporary events - the social and political events of the period which inform the text.
  - The life of the writer - the personal events and circumstances of the writer which inform the text.
  - Setting - the places or institutions which are featured in the novel.

Film and TV adaptations

These offer immediate period ambience but sometimes take liberties with the text.

Period artefacts

Songs and music of the period may be available from the school's music department or the local library. Photographs, objects, paintings and costume books can be borrowed from libraries, and local museums often keep boxes of artefacts for hands-on work with schools.

Other literary stimuli include diaries, letters, posters or menus all of which can be revealing. Students might simply be posed the question, 'What do these reveal to you about the society that produced them?'

FIG 37 A scene from *Jane Eyre* (with Timothy Dalton as Rochester)

CHAPTER 4

Encounters with older literature

PROMOTING OLDER LITERATURE

If students are to feel comfortable with older literature, and familiar with its language, then it is important for them to meet it early in their school career and to maintain contact. Whilst there is not the time to devote long teaching spells to older literature, it is possible to promote it throughout the year.

A WRITER WEEK

A writer week focuses on one particular author and puts on events and displays for the whole school. You might for example choose Robert Louis Stevenson, Sir Arthur Conan Doyle, William Blake, Thomas Hardy or Christina Rossetti. Your programme for the week might include:

- reading one poem at the start of certain lessons
- a choral reading of one poem by a class in assembly
- a range of poems displayed around the school, enlarged and laminated
- a display area in the library focusing on the writer's life with books on loan
- a session devoted to the close reading of a gripping poem or passage
- a notice board display

A termly focus on one writer would introduce 15 writers in the span of a secondary student's time at school. Responsibility for organising the weeks might be delegated to a new member of department or rotated among the staff.

LUNCHTIME READINGS

Lunchtime readings lasting no more than thirty minutes can be organised periodically with guest readers (members of staff, parents, older pupils) who perform their favourite poems or extracts. Students are encouraged to see that people other than English teachers enjoy literature.

PROFESSIONAL READERS

There are professional performers who give excellent dramatised readings of Chaucer or Dickens, although they can be costly.

SHOWING THE CLASSIC SERIAL

Capitalise on current films and TV series based on classic texts by featuring the text, author and related literature in a display.

PRE-20TH CENTURY OR CLASSICS BOOK BOX

Select attractive looking texts to create a 'Classics' book box from which pupils may borrow. Avoid dusty and dreary copies. Borrowing from the box appeals to students; it has cachet.

A book box on Dickens, for example might include the following:
Great Expectations - 5 copies
Great Expectations (abridged) - 5 copies
Oliver Twist - 5 copies
Oliver Twist (abridged) - 5 copies
A Charles Dickens Selection - 10 copies
A Christmas Carol - 5 copies
The Christmas Books - 5 copies
David Copperfield - 3 copies
Hard Times - 2 copies

A mixed classical prose box might contain 3 or 4 copies each of:
Dr Jekyll and Mr Hyde
Frankenstein
Dracula
Treasure Island
Silas Marner
Jane Eyre
Northanger Abbey
Sherlock Holmes Stories
The Wessex Tales
Tales by Edgar Allan Poe

HOLIDAY READING LIST

Issue a reading list prior to the Christmas and the Summer holidays. These are the times when people are willing to buy books as Christmas presents or for holiday reading, and parents often appreciate guidance.

LIBRARY PROMOTION

Ask the school librarian to give special emphasis to older texts in displays, promotions and reading lists.

CHOOSING TEXTS

Despite the constraints of the budget, the stock cupboard and the examination syllabus, departments will wish to choose texts which are interesting and accessible, and which promote positive role models. At the same time we need to introduce students to increasingly challenging literature whilst allowing them to balance their reading diet with more lightweight texts.

Here are our own recommendations. These are texts we have used successfully with children of a variety of ages, abilities and inclinations.

SHORT STORIES

Short stories can provide a useful introduction to older prose texts as well as being a literary form worthy of study in their own right. Although they are brief, the language can tend to be compacted and rather dense. This is particularly true of Victorian short stories. Extracts can be valuable but there is a danger of fragmenting a pupil's experience of literature.

Below is a list of our top ten stories. Many of these stories fit comfortably into units on genre such as horror, science-fiction, romance and crime and this may be a helpful way of introducing them alongside more modern texts in a meaningful context.

1. **The Speckled Band** One of the Sherlock Holmes stories by Arthur Conan Doyle which has a good puzzle in it.

2. **The Hound of the Baskervilles** Another Sherlock Holmes adventure by Conan Doyle. Tackle this and the other stories with humour and melodrama, and they will go down well.

3. **The Withered Arm by Thomas Hardy** A substantial story which is easily 'edited', and has a number of vivid key scenes which excite the imagination.

4. **Tony Kytes – The Arch Deceiver by Thomas Hardy** Another accessible story.

5. **The Signalman by Charles Dickens** A short ghost story which starts slowly but builds effectively. You can read it all in class and get plenty of work out of it.

6. **The Stolen Bacillus by H. G. Wells** An accessible science fiction story with a sting in the tale.

7. **The Tell Tale Heart by Edgar Allan Poe** A tale to capture the imagination and sit comfortably alongside modern counterparts.

8. **The Pavilion on the Links by Robert Louis Stevenson** Shivering sands, cloak-and-dagger villains, treasure chests, a secret romance and derring-do! Teach it with a sense of fun.

9. **The Unexpected by Kate Chopin** A romance with an unexpected feminist slant. Works well in a unit with modern romance stories.

10. **The Black Cat by Edgar Allan Poe** A grisly tale which, not surprisingly appeals to readers at both key stages!

NOVELS

On the whole, we think you should choose the novel you enjoy best. A novel is a huge investment of time and energy, and enthusiasm counts for a great deal. However, our top ten would include:

The Mayor of Casterbridge by Thomas Hardy Traditional KS4 text. Easy to prune as you go, with obvious 'set piece' highlights.

Far from the Madding Crowd by Thomas Hardy Traditionally an A-level text, this can be made accessible. The film is dated but still rather good.

Hard Times by Charles Dickens One of the shortest of Dickens' novels, but rather bleak. The TV version starring Bob Peck is excellent but similarly dour. There are some unexpected openings for drama in the tense relationships and the dilemmas faced by the characters.

Great Expectations by Charles Dickens A favourite text with its gallery of characters, moods and colourful scenes. There are at least three good films to compare.

Oliver Twist by Charles Dickens The advantage is students' previous knowledge (a mixed blessing if they have seen a musical version). The disadvantage is that it is an early and unsophisticated work.

Pride and Prejudice by Jane Austen The paradigm love story. The 1996 BBC serial boosts the level of male interest.

Northanger Abbey by Jane Austen The shortest and earliest of Austen's novels. One good TV adaptation (BBC), and recommended to schools who study the Gothic horror in KS3.

Silas Marner by George Eliot An accessible and compelling storyline. One excellent TV adaptation starring Ben Kingsley and Patsy Kensit.

Jane Eyre by Charlotte Brontë First person narrative and an accessible storyline. Several good, recent film versions. Challenges traditional notions of romance.

Treasure Island by Robert Louis Stevenson Particularly accessible at Key Stage 3. Many colourful characters who will be familiar to students.

POETRY

There are numerous poets who are accessible at both key stages if approached sensibly, but you need to be selective. Try some of the following.

William Blake

Deceptively simple, the poems allow for differentiated questions. Use Blake's own illustrations.

- The Tyger
- The Clod and the Pebble
- The Poison Tree
- London
- Extracts from the Proverbs of Heaven and Hell.

John Keats

Rich in imagery and teaching opportunities. Teach Keats in High Summer!

- La Belle Dame sans Merci
- Isabella or The Pot of Basil
- Ode on Melancholy
- To Autumn
- Meg Merrilees

William Wordsworth

Best placed in context. Use in tandem with sister Dorothy's diaries about the incidents which informed *Beggars* and *Daffodils*.

- Composed upon Westminster Bridge
- Simon Lee
- Daffodils
- Beggars
- The skating extract from The Prelude

Robert Browning

Poems which lend themselves to reading aloud.

- How they brought the good news from Aix to Ghent
- The Pied Piper of Hamelin
- Evelyn Hope
- Porphyria's Lover
- My Last Duchess

Percy Bysshe Shelley

An acquired taste. Try and see.

- Ozymandias
- A Song
- Song to the Men of England
- The Cold Earth Slept Below

John Clare

Poignant, plain poems – an antidote to Victorian pomposity.

- Hedgehog
- The Pale Sun
- I Am
- Love Lies Beyond the Tomb

Christina Rossetti

Her poems are lyrical and are often tinged with images of spurned love, death and remembrance. The language makes them accessible at both key stages.

- Goblin Market
- Song
- Cousin Kate
- In the Round Tower at Jhansi
- Up-hill

Tennyson

His longer, more narrative poems are quite accessible at both key stages.

- The Charge of the Light Brigade
- Mariana
- The Lady of Shalott

Hardy

Hardy often writes about lost love. His poems are more widely used at Key Stage 4, but the Satires of Circumstance poems are excellent for Key Stage 3.

- Beeny Cliff
- The Place on the Map
- The Darkling Thrush
- Poems from the Satires of Circumstance (At the Drapers, At Tea, The Ruined Maid, In the Moonlight, and In Church)

Shakespeare

Try some of the sonnets.

- Shall I compare thee to a summer's day?
- Let me not to the marriage of true minds
- My mistress' eyes are nothing like the sun
- When I do count the clock

DRAMA

Shakespeare's plays are rich and well-resourced and most could be tackled with a little imagination at either key stage although some, such as *Hamlet* and *Measure for Measure* work especially well if kept until the sixth form. Favourites tend to be, with good reason:

Macbeth

Possibly the most used Shakespeare play at Key Stage 4, and now a set text for Key Stage 3. The Polanski film has not dated and the students love it!

The Merchant of Venice

Fast growing in its popularity at Key Stage 4, the play deals with uncomfortable issues of anti-Semitism. Thoughtful students will enjoy the challenge.

A Midsummer Night's Dream

This play was used at Key Stage 3 as a result of the Shakespeare tests but it works equally well at Key Stage 4.

Romeo and Juliet

This play was much used at Key Stage 3 for the Shakespeare tests but you will find that the extra year of maturity helps students to cope with its emotional issues at Key Stage 4.

The Tempest

A magical play which works surprisingly well with younger students. Set them the task of how to present the opening storm on stage!

Twelfth Night

An accessible comedy. The recent film version starring Imogen Stubbs is lively and imaginative. Now a set text for Key Stage 3.

There are many older plays by other playwrights which are worth a fresh look:

She Stoops to Conquer by Oliver Goldsmith

The language is surprisingly accessible and the humour is rich. The play is often performed regionally.

Dr Faustus by Christopher Marlowe

A demanding play but the image of the man who sold his soul to the devil may well intrigue your more thoughtful students.

The Rivals by R. B. Sheridan

A comedy in a similar vein to *She Stoops to Conquer* but not quite as accessible.

Pygmalion by G. B. Shaw

A favourite with many teachers. It raises language issues which can have a rich spin-off in the classroom.

ILLUSTRATED EDITIONS

Our favourites include:

The Rime of the Ancient Mariner by Samuel Taylor Coleridge

Illustrations by Gustav Dore
Published by Dover Books, an American company.

Hiawatha by Longfellow

Illustrations by Susan Jeffers
A Picturemac from Macmillan.

The Canterville Ghost by Oscar Wilde

Illustrations by Lizbeth Zwerger
A Picture Book Studio.

The Selfish Giant by Oscar Wilde

Illustrations by Lizbeth Zwerger
A Picture Book Studio.
Although you might think of this as too junior, the illustrations are rather adult featuring a 'giant' who is a large but ordinary man.

Goblin Market by Christina Rossetti

Illustrations by Martin Ware
Gollancz.

East O' the Sun and West O' the Moon by Dasent

Illustrations by P. J. Lynch
Walker Books.
This traditional Norwegian fairy tale was translated into English in 1856. The translation has merits of its own.

Alice in Wonderland by Lewis Carroll

Original illustrations by the author
Everyman.

William Blake

A selection of accessible poems illustrated by some of his most wonderful paintings and watercolours
Aurum Press.

Other pre-C20 poets in this illustrated series include Elizabeth Barrett Browning, Byron, Donne, Hardy, Keats, Longfellow, Poe, Rossetti, Shakespeare and Shelley, but of course the illustrations are less pertinent, not being by the authors.

Beowulf

Kevin Crossley Holland & Charles Keeping
Oxford.
Stunning illustrations and high-quality modernised prose.